MATH, MANIPULATIVES, and MAGIC WANDS

By

"The Bag Ladies"

Karen Simmons and Cindy Guinn

Illustrated by

Cindy Guinn

Maupin House

Math, Manipulatives, & Magic Wands
Copyright © 2001 Karen Simmons and Cindy Guinn
Illustrated by Cindy Guinn

Book design and layout: Cindy Guinn
Photographs: Courtesy of Donna Purtell

Library of Congress Cataloging-in-Publication Data

Simmons, Karen, 1948-
   Math, manipulatives, & magic wands : manipulatives, literature ideas, and hands-on
 math activities for the K-5 classroom / Karen Simmons and Cindy Guinn ; illustrated by
 Cindy Guinn.
     p. cm.
Includes bibliographical references.
ISBN 0-929895-49-5
   1. Mathematics--Study and teaching (Elementary) I. Title : math, manipulatives, and
 magic wands. II. Guinn, Cindy, 1959- III. Title.

QA1135.6 .S56 2001
 372.7--dc21

                                                                      2001044510

Also by the Bag Ladies:
 A Bookbag of the Bag Ladies' Best
 Bags, Boxes, Buttons, & Beyond

ISBN-10: 0-929895-49-5
ISBN-13: 978-0-929895-49-9

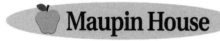 **Maupin House**

Maupin House Publishing, Inc.
2416 NW 71st Place
Gainesville, FL 32653

1-800-524-0634 / 352-373-5588
352-373-5546 (fax)
www.maupinhouse.com
info@maupinhouse.com

Publishing Professional Resources that Improve Classroom Performance

10 9 8 7

DEDICATION

To my wonderful parents: my dad, Jesse Muir, who was an engineer and tried to instill a love of math in me; and my mom, Betty Muir, who instilled the belief in me to keep on trying. K.S.

To my special parents: Tom and Mary Salopek, who only thought they retired until they became the Bag Ladies' Shipping and Handling Department. Thanks for "handling" another job well done!   C.G.

SPECIAL THANKS TO

Donna Purtell, a creative, patient, and talented photographer and friend

All of our students who found **math** to be fun to learn with **manipulatives** and, of course,
a bit of magic

WELCOME

Dear Educator,

It is with great pride that we introduce you to our second book: *Math, Manipulatives, and Magic Wands*. We are teachers first, and it is through the love of teaching that we started writing thematic units with hands-on activities for teachers to follow, with literature to enhance the unit and motivate students. These units, (in a bag), allowed us to present make-n-take workshops throughout Florida and eventually other states, getting teachers excited about teaching. Our first book, *A Bookbag of the Bag Ladies Best*, was a culmination of the literature, hands-on projects, and Bag Lady ideas that helped students of all abilities learn in a fun way.

And now you've asked us to write a book for teaching math. Once again, we have combined great literature with student projects, but this time we have used manipulatives in teaching the skills of math and the standards of the National Council of Teachers of Mathematics. We have included photos, drawings, and step-by-step directions for making math relevant to all students.

Being teachers has helped us write this book for you, making it teacher-friendly and student achievable. We hope that you enjoy our ongoing "story" of the Bag Ladies' teaching styles.

Remember, we wrote this book together, but we do some things differently in our own classrooms. We have different strengths, and we truly believe that we work well together because we share our abilities. As in our workshops we tell stories about each other. You may hear about those stories in this book told by one or the other of us.

Lastly, what is the magic? To us it is the fact that we have a lot of years of teaching between us, and the "magic" of enjoying teaching is still there. What has caused this in the teaching of math? A hands-on approach, a no-risk learning classroom, and of course, a magic wand.

May your wishes come true for all your math students.
Love,
The Bag Ladies

Table of Contents

PART I

Math, Manipulatives, and Magic Wands 11

    Why Math, Manipulatives, and Magic Wands? 11

    How, When, and Where Do I Use This Book? 14

    Math Vocabulary 15

    Estimation 22

    Munching Math 24

    Math Journals 25

    Math Games 27

    Domino Math 30

    Playing Card Math 32

    Grids, Charts, Venn Diagrams, and More 34

    Suggested Literature 38

    Math Literature 40

    Other Math-related Literature 42

PART II

Math Manipulative Projects 43

    Project Page Set-up 46

    Abacus Bracelet 48

    Bean Bug Counters 50

    Black Dot Counting 52

    Business Card Facts 54

    Calculator Riddles 56

    Candy Bar Fractions 58

    CD Case Math 60

    Clocks and Shadows 62

    Coin Time Lines 64

    Counting Rhyme Books 66

    Fact Sticks 68

    Folder Frame Problems 70

    Geometry Quilts 72

    Googol Necklace 74

    Hefty Plate Math 76

    Hundred Penny Boxes 78

    M&M Math 80

    Make Your Own Tangrams 82

    Manipulative Manager 84

    Math Fact Necklace 86

    Math Wallets 88

    My Math Dream 90

    Name Game 92

    Napier Bones 94

    Number Stamps 96

Origami Book 98
Paper Clip Circumference 100
Pattern Pockets 102
Percent Grids 104
Spaghetti Lines 106
Spend a Million 108
Symmetry Paint Picture 110
Velcro Math Poems 112

PART III
The Magic of Pulling It All Together **114**
Folder Holder 116
ABC Book 118
Math Literature Reports 120
Math Journaling 122
Magic Wands 124

Math Blackline Masters . . . .
Dominoes 128
Playing Card Math 131
Mancala Board 132
Estimating 133
Problem Solving 134
Candy Bar Fractions 135
CD Case 137
Clocks and Shadows 139
Coin Timeline 140
Counting Book 141
Quilt Square 144
M & M Math 146
Create a Tangram Story 148
Math Wallet 149
My Amazing Math Deam 150
Napier Bones 151
Pattern Pocket 152
Percent Pattern Grid Paper 153
Spend a Million 154
Math and Literature 155-156

A-B-C Book Blackline Masters **157-184**

About the Authors **185**

Math, Manipulatives, and Magic Wands

WHY MATH, MANIPULATIVES, AND MAGIC WANDS?

As teachers, we all know that the criteria for assessing math have changed in the last few years. Students are asked to solve problems and to write *how* they solved the problem in a clear concise way. This, we are finding, is not an easy task for all students.

As you look over your classes, the faces of your students say it all! There sit a few students eager and excited for a challenging year of math. They love math! It comes easy to them and they solve the same problem three different ways.

Then you have the average students who like math, work hard at it, read and reread the problems, and raise their hands to "take a risk" explaining how they arrived at their answers.

Finally, you have blank faces sometimes displaying the tiniest hint of fear, but mostly trying to shrink into their desks to avoid a trip to the board or a verbal confrontation. They read and reread the problem. You read the problem to them, stressing the clues or key words, and still their faces are blank!

Is this familiar to you? Probably so. As a teacher you take it personally that each of your students, no matter what their strengths and weaknesses, progress to their highest achievement level possible with *your* help. And, in today's high stakes performance climate, it's even more important to make sure that all your students comprehend the language and operations of math. This book helps you achieve that goal. And, it goes a step further: Your students not only will perform better, but they'll have fun while learning!

Our years of teaching have shown us that "hands-on" is the key to student progress in math. Manipulatives allow students to "see" the actual working of a problem from start to finish. They help many of those blank faces to truly comprehend the process behind each problem.

Here's a personal memory that remains vivid in my mind. My dad, an engineer, is helping me with my homework, specifically the dreaded story-problem solving. As you might guess, I was one of those "blank faces."

"I've explained this five times," he'd remind me, in a fatherly way. "How can you not *get* it?" he'd implore. And I'd think to myself that it would take "magic" for me to work this problem!

That's why when Cindy suggested we write a book on the topic of math, I was not too excited, to say the least. Once again, I felt it would take more than a sprinkle of magic to get me motivated to write and create math projects.

As teachers, we knew that our students had to be proficient in using critical thinking skills to solve a problem, as well as able to *write* to explain their reasoning. How could we help teachers who had students like me in their classes? We also wanted to help K-5 teachers be aware of the standards, processes, and applications needed to build skills year to year, using a hands-on approach to learning for *all* students. Those were our goals—or should we say, "challenges?"

To achieve these goals we concentrated on connecting literature and vocabulary to the NCTM standards and adding the key component of fun in the form of hands-on manipulative projects. We then taught the students how to write about their thinking processes.

Hey, this was getting better! Literature, writing, vocabulary, projects to help teach math? I can *do* this! And so could our students! But they would need just the slightest touch of one more ingredient...magic!

In this book, we introduce some math literature to motivate your math classes, suggest math vocabulary needed for assessment to help students use the language of math in their writing, and demonstrate make-n-take projects as manipulatives to make the skills visual and fun! Because we are teachers first, we know that you need to *see* this magic act. Will rabbits appear? No, but your students will become math masters without too much abracadabra.

HOW, WHEN, AND WHERE DO I USE THIS BOOK?

We have divided the book into three parts. In Part 1 we present areas of the K-5 math curriculum. Most of these skills will be presented yearly, building upon one another and adding degrees of difficulty.

Part 2 demonstrates the manipulatives that students can make, reinforcing the skills learned and allowing them to see the operation. These activities are presented in an easy step-by-step format with a photograph of each finished project. We have added the National Council of Teachers of Mathematics (NCTM) standards that each activity supports. We also add a few Bag Lady magic touches in the form of extension activities. A suggested children's trade book is proposed for each skill/activity that correlates reading with math and gets students excited about the activity.

Part 3 contains the blackline copy sheets to make it easy for you to present hands-on projects to students. Other blackline copy sheets included are A to Z Vocabulary for either primary or intermediate-aged students. On these sheets students learn the language of math as they define math vocabulary words correlated to their skill level.

As you teach each standard for your grade level, combine a hands-on activity project once a week for students to manipulate a particular skill. You may also combine the activity of using one or two letters of the suggested alphabet words per week in order to present a variety of math skills that introduce math vocabulary.

MATH VOCABULARY

Do you know what a googol is? A.) the first words of a newborn. B.) a bird somewhat like the extinct dodo. C.) a 1 followed by one hundred zeros, or D.) a Hungarian dish of meat and gravy.

If you guessed C.) you are right. Oh, if only the testing that your students will be required to take could be that easy!

Learning math vocabulary can be fun for students if they can see the word, use the word, and make a project to apply the word to their learning of math skills.

We recommend that all K-5 teachers display math vocabulary in their classrooms. Encourage students to use this vocabulary when they speak and write to explain how they solve story problems. Here are some ways in which a teacher may do this:

- Have students create classroom posters illustrating math vocabulary words and their meanings.
- Display math word walls.
- Make Math ABC books with illustrations and definitions.
- Make math games to practice vocabulary. (Jeopardy)
- Ask students to use math vocabulary in their math journals when explaining "how" they solved a problem.
- Create math dictionaries.

Review the vocabulary introduced year to year, so that the student is constantly building upon previous math vocabulary.

Math Vocabulary Grades K-1

more	greater than	triangle	subtract	before
less	add	rectangle	are left	after
circle	less than	hundred	whole	between
least	equal to	sum	half	biggest
half	one more	addition	short	smallest
tall	one less	plus	longer	sphere
penny	same as	in all	shorter	cube
nickel	ones	all	fewest	cone
dime	tens	together	same	cylinder
quarter	equal	subtraction	thirds	sides
cent	square	minus	fourths	corners

Math Vocabulary Grades 2/3

dollar	rows of	tenth	centimeter
decimal	equal	fair share	pound
hundreds	groups	numerator	kilogram
regroup	divide	denominator	length
greater than	multiple	fraction	width
less than	times	rectangular solid	odd
equal to	multiplication	edge	even
difference	fourth	face	estimation
groups of	third	inch	addend

More Math Vocabulary Grades 2/3

product	kilometer	thousands	a.m.
quotient	cup	parallelogram	p.m.
factor	pint	temperature	perpendicular
dividend	quart	hexagon	lines
divisor	gallon	octagon	area
equivalent	liter	polygon	units
feet	ounce	quadrilateral	square units
yard	gram	parallel lines	cubic units
mile	degrees	symmetry	

Math Vocabulary Grades 4/5

hundredth	a little more than	acute angle
decimal	symmetry	degree
fraction	congruent	right angle
million	linear unit of measurement	obtuse angle
angle	line	rounding
hundred	line segment	close to
thousand	ray	factor
ten thousand	intersecting line	approximately
close to	improper fraction	greatest common factor

More Math Vocabulary Grades 4/5

whole number	hundred million	ten-thousandths
average	almost as much as	decagon
mean	about the same	pentagon
median	about half	rhombus
mode	more than half	trapezoid
meter	billions	parallelogram
millimeter	tenths	compass
ten	hundredths	protractor
million	thousandths	center

More Math Vocabulary Grades 4/5

diameter	square inches	cubic centimeter
radius	square feet	cubic meter
chord	square yards	
circumference	square	
equilateral	centimeter	
triangle	square meters	
scalene triangle	cubic inches	
isosceles triangle	cubic foot	
reciprocal	cubic yard	

ESTIMATION

Our students love to guess the answers, especially when it has to do with their teacher! How old am I? How many children do you think I have? How old do you think they are? The answers are sometimes cute and many times alarming! That old?

So many times we see students stare at a jar full of objects and just "pull a number from the air" to guess the amount. It is our job as teachers to *teach* students to make accurate or careful guesses to predict a number of items. We try to give the students tools to use as they carefully predict what might be a close-to-accurate estimate.

A good way to motivate students for a lesson on estimation is to share the book, *Betcha,* by Stuart J. Murphy, in which two boys enter a guessing contest about the number of candies in a jar. On the way to the store, the author shows the reader how one of the boys accurately predicts people on the bus, cars in the traffic, and finally the items in the jar. Students are always amazed at the reasoning the boy uses and that there really is some thinking involved in the estimating process.

To introduce this concept in our own classroom, we start by providing our own "estimating jar." It can be filled with marbles, pennies, rice, beans, macaroni, balls, jacks, peanuts, erasers, pebbles, buttons, cereal, popcorn, dice, blocks, seashells, gumballs, candies, pasta, beads, jelly beans, nuts, bolts, washers, raisins, Gummy Bears, pretzel nuggets, sunflower seeds, crayons, or any other objects.

Next, we allow students to observe the jar for a few days. During this time, we ask creative questions for morning work on the board, which helps the students use critical thinking skills to make an accurate guess. These questions would be grade-level appropriate: How many tens do you think the container holds, or

22

how many of these objects could you hold in a handful? How many handfuls would fill the container?

At the end of the week, students are asked to write their estimates in their math journals and explain the thinking process used to make these guesses.

The class should count the items in the jar together. We recommend that the items be divided into groups for ease of counting.

Finally, the students are asked to record the correct number of objects in their math journals and compare this count to their own estimates, discussing how they had arrived at their estimate.

A GREAT FOLLOW-UP TO THIS ACTIVITY IS...Students bring in their own estimating jar of objects. Give them a date that their jar is due, so that each week a jar is available for estimating. The students are given extra credit for preparing the jar. They love to try and come up with unique items for the jar, especially if it does not use food items.

WE USE ESTIMATING JAR GUESS PAPERS to make this activity neat and special for the students. (See Estimating Blackline #4)

These jars can be kept for future years and make a great colorful display at your math center.

This idea can be expanded into a school-wide math activity. Set up jars so that all students may participate in the estimation process. This might be done in the media center where all students visit sometime during the week. Jars can be set up for each grade level. Winners, estimating the closest number of items in the jar would be announced at the end of the week.

MUNCHING MATH

Food is an old "magic trick" to help motivate students. Using food as a manipulative with math problems is an activity that, when combined with great literature, makes for some "yummy" projects. Whether you are using M&M's, Hershey bars, or Skittles, the activity is sweet! You might decide to use Cheerios or pretzel sticks, and you won't be surprised to find that there is a story for all of these great "math munchers."

We have included a blackline using both M&M's and Hershey bars. (See Candy Bar Fractions Blackline # 6 and M & M Math Blackline #12). Your students will enjoy performing math operations using these manipulatives, especially when they are asked to eat the leftovers. Magically, the operations of division and multiplication are mastered as the student builds his own sets of candies or divides the Cheerios into groups. Even fractions aren't tricky when the class uses candy bars to learn about numerators and denominators.

Students love to think of their own food items for the class and to write their own "munching books" for classroom publishing. What a great way to incorporate math skills, writing directions, and following directions into one creative student-made book!

Don't forget to use pretzel sticks and cheese when working with geometry, or noodles when forming geometric shapes.

But, don't stop there! For example, food manipulatives also allow students to predict the cost of the candy bars used and explaining ways to find the cost of the purchase for the class.

However you choose to use food items with your math students, we know that it will be a great way to "gobble up" facts!

MATH JOURNALS

Assessments now ask students to use math vocabulary and critical thinking skills to verbalize the thinking process they go through to solve a problem. Obviously, the earlier they start this process the more adept they become in their skill of writing to explain.

To make this activity fun and challenging to the students of all grades, we suggest that students make their own math journals and practice this writing and thinking skill daily. The math journal is a new concept for many teachers, especially in primary grades. In the early grades students may draw pictures to explain their thinking process in solving math concepts of adding and subtracting, sorting, graphing and other grade specific skills. As students become more adept at writing, they may explain their thinking process using the vocabulary learned with the skills taught. Here's one way to use the journals with your students to obtain better math scores and improved narrative and expository writing.

Students take out their journals, read the Problem of the Day on the overhead, at their seat, or on the board, and after showing their work to solve the problem, they explain in writing or drawing the steps they took to arrive at their answer. Students can use transition words as *first, then,* and *finally* as they explain the steps. For some variety, they may write a narrative math piece once a week, for example, What I Would Do with a Million Dollars.

Again, we suggest making it fun for the students by assigning points for correct answers. Allow them to keep their points for the week, announcing first and second winners at the end of the week, stamping correct answers with special stamps or stickers, and/or having students take turns being "the teacher" and explaining how they solved the daily problem.

Hint: Before pursuing any of these activities, we suggest spending about a week modeling the correct way to explain their work with the appropriate vocabulary. Refer to the Problem Solving Blackline #5.

MATH GAMES

Our years of teaching have shown us that "hands-on" is the key to student progress in math. Manipulatives allow students to "see" the actual working of a problem from start to finish.

Games are an important manipulative. What better way to learn critical thinking skills than to play the game of mancala, or practice addition skills by playing dominoes? Playing card games also helps students at a young age manipulate numbers. Whether adding, subtracting, sorting, or comparing, a deck of cards gets students working with numbers while playing a card game.

The best part of using games in math is that your students will make the games they play. Just a few everyday materials "magically" change a struggling student into a game designer with a math skill focus.

MANCALA is an ancient game of strategy and mathematical ability that students love to play. We have students bring in egg cartons to make their own games. They cut off the lid of the carton and cut the lid in half. Students sit across from each other with the six holes of the carton facing each player. They place the lids at either end of the playing "board." The lid on the player's right is his home lid. Each cup contains three stones (flat glass-like colored pebbles used to anchor plants work very well).

There are many variations to the playing of this game but we like the version shown here. The object of the game is to accumulate the most stones in your home lid. Players begin by placing three stones in each of their egg carton cups. Player 1 picks up all the stones in any cup on his side. He then distributes one in each pit—moving in a counterclockwise direction—including his own home lid if he has enough stones. He does not put any in his opponent's home lid at any time during the game. As he distributes the stones, if the last stone lands in an empty pit on his side, he may "capture" his opponent's stones in the pit directly across from his by picking these up and placing them and that last stone in his own home lid. If he ever lands his last stone in his home lid, he gets a free turn. Player 1's turn is over when he makes a capture, lands his last stone in one of his opponent's cups, or he lands his last stone in a cup on his side that does not permit a capture.

Player 2 now repeats the procedure above, beginning by picking up all the stones in one pit on his side.

The game is over when all six cups on one side are empty. The player with stones remaining places them in his home lid. The player with the greatest number of stones is the winner.

Hint: Teach mancala by making a transparency of (Mancala Board Blackline #3) and use bingo chips or overhead markers to demonstrate the rules and procedures.

To add some magic: Use seashells, gemstones, buttons, or beans as markers. Most of all have fun using math skills!

DOMINOES-We first saw dominoes at a Dollar Store and thought, "What a great idea! Let's buy a pack for each student and let them play math games for morning work." *Wrong!* What do students love to use dominoes for? *Right!* And our objective was not in building "domino trails" for falling over. So, because we thought the game was a great one, and we knew students loved to make their own games, we now use fun foam for the actual dominoes and apply the dots with black permanent sharp markers. Now, each student has his own set of *quiet* dominoes. Two players would use one set of these dominoes. You win if you are the first to play all of your tiles.

The dominoes are mixed up and laid facedown. Each player takes seven dominoes. The person with the highest number on the domino goes first. Players take turns adding tiles. They add up all dots on their tile to get their score. If they cannot move,

they must choose one from the extra pile and keep on picking up dominoes until a play can be made. You win if you get up to a certain number of points decided before the game begins.
Hint: Make a transparency from (Domino Blackline #1A, #1B, and #1C) to teach the entire class how to play the game.
To add some magic: Have students design envelopes for their dominoes.

PLAYING CARDS-Using a deck of playing cards, students can show how many ways they can create certain numbers. They may deal a certain number of cards and try to create bar graphs by arranging the cards from smallest to largest or by suits. Students also may practice addition and subtraction or even multiplication.

To help your students use the cards independently, we have designed a cardholder so that the cards do not slip around on the desks and land where so many manipulatives have a habit of landing, on the floor. (See Playing Card Math Blackline #2)
Hint: Many casinos will supply teachers with old (used few times) playing cards for their classrooms.
To add some magic: Keep a lost-and-found box in the classroom in which to place any manipulatives found after cleanup.

CD CASE MATH GAMES- Empty CD cases make excellent storage cases for student-designed games. With just a bit of magnetic metal, which can be purchased in sheets or strips, the student can create a magnetic game within the case. We have started you with two of our games. (See CD Case Blackline #7, Page 1 and 2)
Hint: Insert magnetic metal in back of the CD case. Place paper game board over the metal. Use magnetic numbers and symbols by attaching magnetic strip to back.
To add some magic: Have each student create a decorative cover to slide under the tabs of the CD case front.

Domino Math

Materials

1. Tagboard or Fun Foam
2. Black fine-tip marker
3. Scissors
4. One zipper-style baggie for domino storage
5. Dominoes
   Blackline 1A-B-C

Extensions

*Domino sets also can be made from card stock paper, construction paper, wood scraps, or watercolor paper. The dots can be put on each domino with crayon, ink pad, marker, paint, or hole punch and construction paper.

Procedures

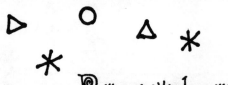

1. Choose one type of paper, wood, or foam and one type of ink, marker or crayon.

2. Each student will need twenty eight rectangles to create a complete set of dominoes. See Blackline master 1 for size and number of dots on each domino.

3. Ask the students to draw dots with black fine-tip markers on each domino until they have completed their sets.

4. Cut dominoes apart with scissors and store in the zipper-style baggie until ready to play a game.

Domino Draw

WINNER-The first to play all of the domino tiles in your pile.

1. Mix up all dominoes face down. Each player takes seven dominoes.

2. The person with the highest number on a domino goes first.

3. Players take turns placing their dominoes to build a chain. You can only play a matching domino. If you don't have a match you must choose another one from the extra pile.

Add the End

WINNER-If you are the first to get 50 points or whatever number agreed upon at start.

1. Mix up all dominoes face down. Each player takes seven dominoes.

2. The person with the highest number of dominos goes first.

3. Players take turns adding tiles to the line. Each time a player adds a tile they add the number of dots to get their score.

4. If a player can not make a move they must take a tile from the extra pile.

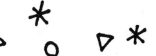

Playing Card Math

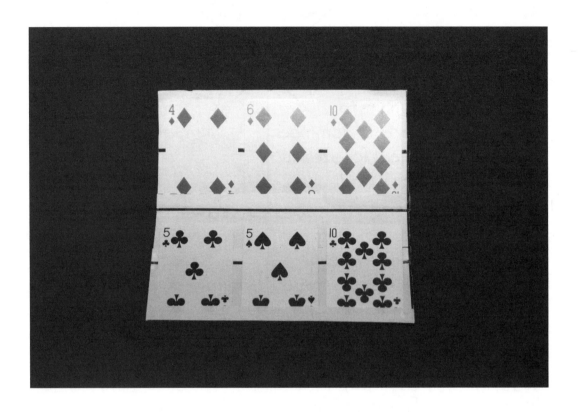

Materials

1. A deck of playing cards (a mini deck works best)
2. Blackline 2 of the playing card holder
3. Scotch tape

Extensions

*Sort the cards by color, suit, or number

*Deal each child a selected number of playing cards. Ask them to create a bar graph using those cards.

Procedures

1. Provide each child with a copy of the blackline master (Blackline can be enlarged to handle regular size playing cards.)

2. Have the child follow the fold lines on the Playing Card Holder blackline as directed.

3. Once all folds are finished tape the ends of each to secure closed to create small pockets.

4. Flip the Playing Card Holder to the backside and tape each fold flat with Scotch tape.

5. The Playing Card Holder is now ready to be used to hold playing cards in place as the children practice creating different math problems and sorting their cards in different ways.

EXAMPLE:
How many different ways can you make a sum of 10? Or any other number up to 12? Use your card holder to display your answers.

Magic Touch

*Students can use their Playing Card Holders to display other types of flash cards, including Business Card flashcards as mentioned in the Manipulative Section of this book.

*Students can make columns on their Playing Card Holders and use them to play Concentration and other games.

NCTM Standards

NUMBERS AND OPERATIONS
Standard-The students will understand numbers, ways of representing numbers, relationships among numbers, and number systems.

ALGEBRA
Standard-The students will understand patterns, relationships, and functions.

PROBLEM SOLVING
Standard-The students will build new mathematical knowledge through problem solving.

GRIDS, CHARTS, VENN DIAGRAMS, AND MORE

Starting in the primary grades, students are asked to compare and contrast, make charts, and graph their findings. Whether done to show simple data collecting (how many students' birthdays are in certain months) or for more complicated data (how many patterns of fingerprints can be seen in a classroom), graphs are tools by which the student assesses information.

In our workshops, we demonstrate to teachers the many methods of making graphs out of simple materials. For example, a simple pull-down shade and some colored duct tape make wonderful grids or bar graphs. The duct tape, which comes in colors, can be used to make the actual grid on the shade or to make circles representing Venn Diagrams. Students can use Post-it notes to put information into the circles.

Today, many of the commercial pocket charts are set up as graphs of different shapes (sometimes in the shape of crayons or trees) and can be used for many graphing activities by filling pockets with colored squares to build the bar graph.

Colored Hefty paper plates work well for demonstrating pie graphs (count the thumb prints around the edges and you'll find 36 for the 360 degrees). When cutting the plates into the center, you will find that they will interlock and turn to represent a pie graph or demonstrate different kinds of angles. You may use up to four different colors of plates giving you ways to teach students about fractions and parts of a circle graph.

Bar Graphs/Line Graphs

_____

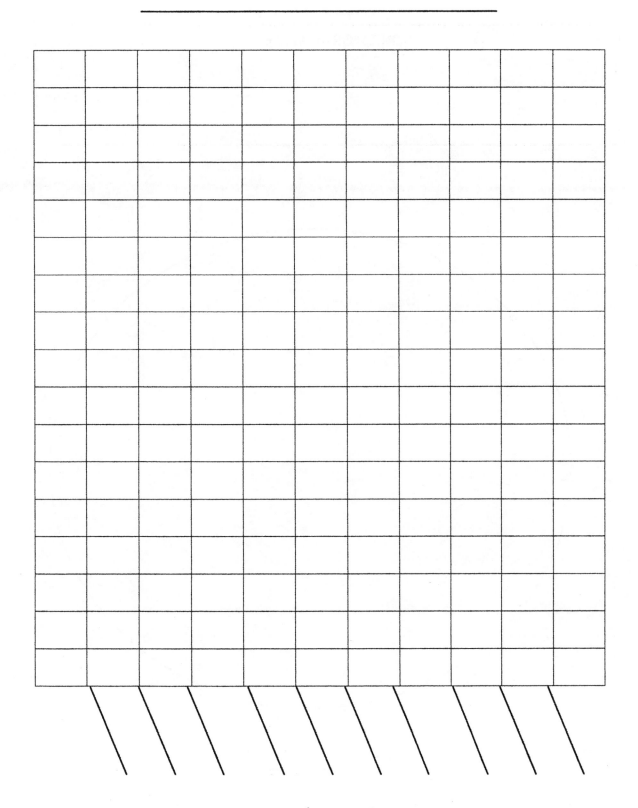

Circle Graphs

CIRCLE GRAPH KEY:

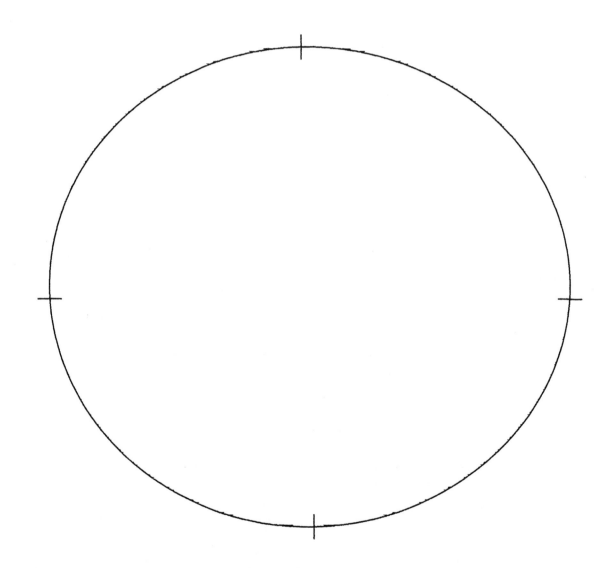

Venn Diagrams

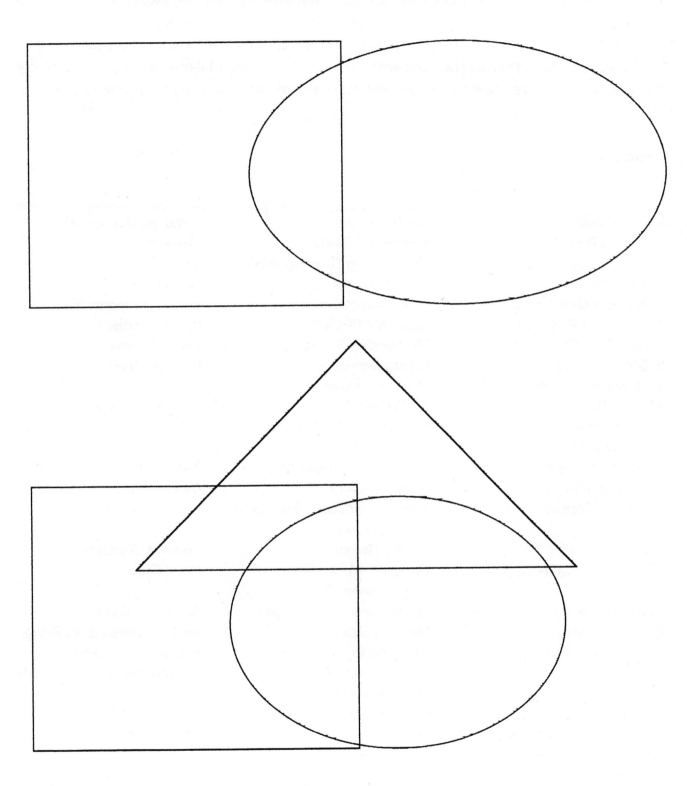

Suggested Literature

With so much good literature that connects math and reading we hesitate to present a list for each of our projects. Each of these hands-on-math activities stands alone to reinforce a particular math skill. For your convenience, we have listed our projects and one literature book that *can* be used with this project. Please keep in mind that these are suggestions only. We know that there are many other books you might choose to use.

PROJECT	BOOK	AUTHOR
1. A-B-C Book	*G is for Googol*	David M. Schwartz
2. Abacus Bracelet	*A String of Beads*	Margarette S. Reid
3. Bean Bug Counters	*The Icky Bug Counting Book*	Jerry Palotta
4. Black Dot Counting	*Ten Black Dots*	Donald Crews
5. Business Card Facts	*Once Upon a Company*	Wendy Anderson Halperin
6. Calculator Riddles	*Calculator Riddles*	David A. Adler
7. Candy Bar Fractions	*The Hershey Bar Fraction Book*	Jerry Palotta
8. CD Math Case	*Mathamusements*	Raymond Blum
9. Clocks and Shadows	*The Grouchy Ladybug*	Eric Carle
10. Coin Timeline	*Get Up and Go*	Stuart J. Murphy
11. Counting Books	*There Were Ten in the Bed*	Child's Play
12. Domino Math	*Domino Addition*	Lynette Long
13. Fact Necklace	*Twelve Ways to Get to Eleven*	Eve Merriam
14. Fact Sticks	*Sunny Numbers*	Carol Crane
15. Folder Frames	*Amazing and Incredible Counting Stories*	Max Grover
16. Folder-Holder	*G is for Googol*	David M. Schwartz
17. Geometry Quilt	*The Quilt Block History of Pioneer Days*	Mary Cobb
18. Googol Necklace	*Can You Count to a Googol?*	Robert E. Wells
19. Hefty Plates	*Skittle Riddles*	Barbara Barbieri McGrath
20. Hundred Penny Box	*The Hundred Penny Box*	Sharon Bell Mathis
21. M&M Math	*M&M Counting Book* *More M&M Math*	Barbara Barbieri McGrath
22. Magic Wands	*Marvelous Math*	Lee Bennett Hopkins
23. Make Your Own Tangrams	*Grandfather Tang's Story*	Ann Tompert
24. Manipulative Manager	*Domino Addition*	Lynette Long
25. Math Journals	*If You Hopped Like A Frog*	David M. Schwartz
26. Math Literature Reports	*A Cloak for a Dreamer*	Aileen Friedman

27. Math Wallets	*Alexander, Who Used to Be Rich Last Sunday*	Judith Viorst
28. My Math Dream	*Amanda Bean's Amazing Dream*	Cindy Neuschwander
29. Name Game	*Counting on Frank*	Rod Clement
30. Napier Bones	*The Amazing Multiplication Book*	Jennie Maizels
31. Number Stamps	*Ready, Set, Hop!*	Stuart J. Murphy
32. Origami Book	*G is for Googol*	David M. Schwartz
33. Paper Clip Circumference	*Sir Cumference and the First Round Table*	Cindy Neuschwander
34. Pattern Pockets	*Picture Pie 2*	Ed Emberley
35. Percent Grids	*Fraction Fun*	David A. Adler
36. Playing Card Math	*Dealing with Addition*	Lynette Long
37. Spaghetti Lines	*The Straight Line Wonder*	Mem Fox
38. Spend a Million	*If You Made a Million*	David M. Schwartz
39. Symmetry Pictures	*The Little Mouse, the Red Ripe Strawberry, and the Big Hungry Bear*	Audrey Woods
40. Velcro Story	*When a Line Bends a Shape Begins*	Rhonda Growler Greene

Math Literature

We begin each new math skill with a story. Enjoy some of our favorite "math literature," stories that introduce a new concept. We know that there are many other great books that deal with math skills; we present just a few suggestions.

Estimating
Betcha
Stuart J. Murphy

Counting on Frank
Rod Clement

Measurement
*Sir Cumference and the
    First Round Table*
Cindy Neuschwander

*Sir Cumference and the
    Dragon of Pi*
Cindy Neuschwander

Ten Beads Tall
Mark Twinn

Money
*Alexander, Who Used to be Rich
    Last Sunday*
Judith Viorst

If You Made a Million
David M. Schwartz

The Buck Book
Anne Akers Johnson

The Hundred Penny Box
Sharon Bell Mathis

Multiplication
Amanda Bean's Amazing Dream
Cindy Neuschwander & Marilyn Burns

A Spooky Set of Multiplication Stories
Loreen Leedy

The Amazing Multiplication Book
Kate Petty & Jennie Maizels

Shapes
A Cloak for the Dreamer
Aileen Friedman

Picture Pie 1 and 2
Ed Emberley

Shape Up!
David Adler

The Straight Line Wonder
Mem Fox

Tangrams
Grandfather Tang's Story
Ann Tompert

The Tortoise Who Bragged
Betsy Franco

Vocabulary
G is for Googol
David M. Schwartz

Math Writing Prompt Ideas

Need a writing prompt for your math vocabulary project activity?
Here are some suggestions that can be mixed and matched.

Write about an invention that makes your life easier.

Create a poem about a piece of candy.

Write about a time you had a problem and describe how you
    solved it.

Write a recipe for your own original pizza.

Write a diamonte-style poem in the shape of a rhombus.

Make an illustration using geometric figures and write about it.

Tell about someone you can always count on and explain how he or
    she helps you.

Explain the step-by-step process used to make something.

Write a poem about your favorite color.

Write a story about an animal named Fibonacci and the things
    he discovers.

Compare yourself to your friend. How are you alike
    and different?

What do you think a googol is? Describe it.

Write a timeline of your day, one hour at a time.

Describe your oldest relative.

Explain how math is used every day.

Write an "if" story about if you could be anyone you wanted to be
    or if you could go anywhere you wanted to go.

Write about a journey to a planet. Who is your guide?

Invent a new number, give it a name, and tell how you chose
    that name.

Write a story about a town with many bridges.

Explain the step-by-step process used in making something.

Explain what makes you happy and what makes you sad.

Other Math-related Literature

Bats on Parade
Kathi Appelt

Bunches and Bunches of Bunnies
Louise Mathews

Bunny Money
Rosemary Wells

Dealing Addition
Lynette Long

Discovering Graph Secrets
Sandra Markle

Double Trouble in Walla Walla
Andrew Clements

How Tall, How Short, How Faraway
David A. Adler

In the Next Three Seconds
Rowland Morgan

Math Curse
Jon Scieszka & Lane Smith

Math for Martians Galaxy Getaway
Jane Tassie & Julie Ferris

Math Start books
Stuart Murphy

On Beyond a Million
David M. Schwartz

Sunny Numbers
Carol Crane

The Greedy Triangle
Marilyn Burns

Math Manipulative Projects

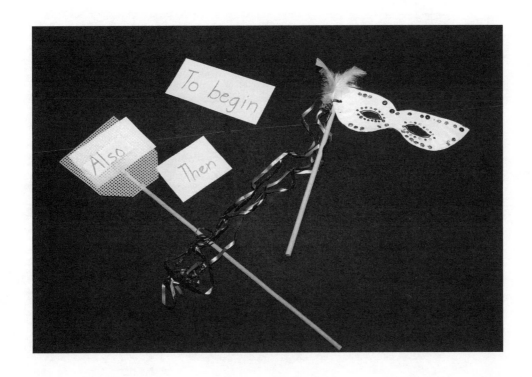

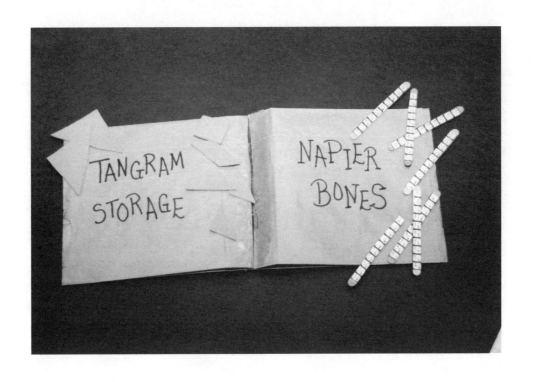

MANIPULATIVES

The words "hands-on," lead us to the main emphasis of Section Two and of the book. Here, we will make the connection in literature, present the materials needed to make the activity, take you through a step-by-step make-n-take of the activity project, present ways to create project extensions, AND correlate it all to the National Council of Teachers of Mathematics (NCTM) Standards. And as if that weren't enough, we will throw in a magic trick or two to make it "sparkle." Now this is MATH that a student can see, hear, and touch!

We are happy to present 48 of our favorite projects to help students learn some of the many skills that they need to master for success standardized tests. We know from experience that all students enjoy learning math in a project-oriented approach. As teachers, we know that you like to see the project, as it would look when completed, so we have included photographs of each of our activities.

We suggest that you make a model and present the project to your students before they create it themselves.

Project Page Set-Up

Photograph of project

Materials

*Materials needed to complete
projects will be listed here.
*Blackline master numbers are
included for easy reference.
*All materials are listed for
one student to complete the
project. Multiply the number
listed by the number of students
in your class.

Extensions

*The ideas listed here are
  ways to extend the project.
*Do not try to do all of
  the listed extensions. Use
  them only when the
  students need more
  practice.

Procedures

Listed on this side of the page will be the steps to complete each project.

Be sure to read over all steps first before attempting to create the project. Often we have include some HINTS or NOTES to assist you when doing these projects with your class.

Blackline masters have been provided for some of the projects if they are needed.

How to use

*We have included some suggestions on how to use the projects. We have tested each one of these in our own classrooms and feel these were very successful.

Magic Touch

This section of each page will share ways that The Bag Ladies make these projects extra special. These ideas often link to other subject areas.

NCTM Standards

NCTM stands for the National Council of Teachers of Mathematics. The standards we have listed are taken from *Principles and Standards for School Mathematics.* We have included these standards to show how standards can still be met while doing creative projects in your classroom.

Abacus Bracelet

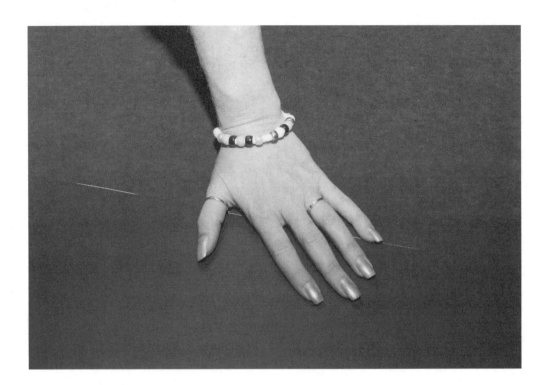

Materials

1. One pipe cleaner
2. Pony beads of various colors

Extensions

* Students can sort beads.
* Create patterns with different colors and types of beads.
* Research the history of beads and their uses.
* Make their own beads.

Procedures

Magic Touch

1. Make a loop in one end of the pipe cleaner just large enough to insert one finger.

2. Twist to secure the loop.

3. String pony beads on the pipe cleaner.

* Students of all ages will enjoy making and using their abacus bracelet.

*Learn about the history of the abacus and its use throughout the world.

*Write about a math invention such as the calculator and discuss how it makes our lives easier.

*Most pony beads are 1/4 inch in width which make them a great quarter-inch ruler.

How to use

* Practice basic facts for addition, subtraction, multiplication, or division.
* Problem-solving problems
* Use bracelets to teach the commutative property.
* Fractions, ratios, percents, patterns, and algebraic thinking can all be practiced using an abacus bracelet.

NCTM Standards

NUMBERS & OPERATIONS
Standard–The students will understand numbers, ways of representing numbers relationships among numbers, and number systems.

ALEGEBRA
Standard–The students will understand patterns, relations, and functions.

PROBLEM SOLVING
Standard–The students will apply and adopt a variety of appropriate strategies to solve problems.

Bean Bug Counters

Materials

1. 10-20 large dry beans (Lima beans or any other large bean)
2. Acrylic paint-various colors
3. Medium-size paint brush
4. Wax paper
5. Storage container to store completed Bean Bug Counters
6. Black fine-tip marker

Extensions

* Use these bugs to create stories.
* Sort bugs by type or color.
* Create a story to go with their bugs.
* Have the students create their own storage containers for their bugs. (See Googol Necklace)

Procedures

1. Lay out the lima beans on wax paper and paint them with the acrylic paint.

2. Allow beans to dry before adding details. Using black fine-tip markers, add detail so each bean resembles an insect. Examples: bumblebee, ladybug, or beetles.

Magic Touch

*Have the students create bugs after reading a book about insects. This will spark both their interest and creativity.

*Limit the children to a small number of bean bugs at first. Add more as needed.

How to use

* Your Bean Bug Containers can be used in place of counters with any type of math problems.

* Students will enjoy sorting, graphing, and classifying their bugs into groups.

* Use bug counters on bar graphs or Venn diagrams to show their characteristics.

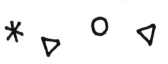

NCTM Standards

NUMBER & OPERATIONS Standard-The students will understand numbers, ways of representing numbers; relationships among numbers, and number systems.

DATA ANALYSIS & PROBABILITY Standard-The students will be able to formulate questions that can be addressed with data and collect, organize, and display relevant data to answer them.

Black Dot Counting

Materials

1. Black dot stickers, found in office supply stores
2. One 12-inch by 18-inch sheet of white drawing paper
3. Crayons, colored pencils, or markers

Extensions

* When students complete their illustrations, create a class book.
* Have older students create individual books to be read and given to younger students.

Procedures

1. Give each student some black dot stickers. They can either choose a number of stickers or you can pass out at random a different number to each child.

2. Instruct the students to use their black dots as part of their illustrations. It is best for them to have an idea of what they want to create before they place their stickers on their paper.

3. Students use their crayons, colored pencils, or markers to draw and color their pictures. When the pictures are completed, students add the black dots. For example: windows of an airplane, dots on a ladybug, or centers to a flower.

4. When all pictures are completed, arrange them by the number of black dots used lowest to the highest number. Bind pictures into a class book and share.

Magic Touch

*Read *Ten Black Dots* by Donald Crews before creating picture. Use the Big Book version if available.

*Brainstorm ideas for pictures before students begin to draw.

5 black dots

NCTM Standards

NUMBERS & OPERATIONS
Standard-The students will understand numbers, ways of representing numbers, relationships among numbers, and number systems.

PROBLEM SOLVING
Standard-The students will apply and adapt a variety of appropriate strategies to solve problems.

Business Card Facts

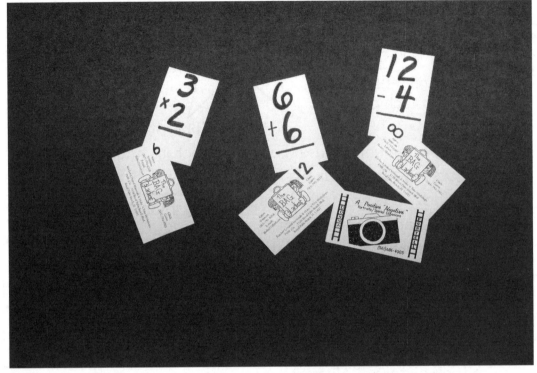

Materials

1. Approximately 20 business cards brought in by students
2. Black fine-tip markers
3. Zipper-style baggie for storage of flashcards

Extensions

*Business cards also can be used to create other types of flashcards for vocabulary, social studies, or science.

*Business cards also can be used to write questions on when creating game boards.

Procedures

1. Give each child 10-20 business cards and a black fine-tip marker.

2. Instruct students to neatly write a math fact problem on the backside of each business card. Do not include the answers to the fact problems.

3. Flip the business card to the front side and write the answer on that side you also can choose not to include the answer on the card at all.

How to use

*These flashcards are easy for even young students to create. Be sure to have the students make a limited number of cards at a time. For example: Fact problems with solutions no greater than five.

*Parents or local businesses usually will be glad to donate business cards to your class for free advertising.

Magic Touch

*Share the story *Once upon a Company* by Wendy Anderson Halperin with your class. Discuss all the different ways math was used in this story.

*Create a business card for the business in the story or for a a business you would like to start some day.

*Write about a business you would like to start some day.

NCTM Standards

Numbers & Operations
Standard-The students will understand meanings of operations and how they relate to one another.

Connections
Standard-The students will recognize and use connections among mathematical ideas.

Standard-The students will recognize and apply mathematics in contexts outside of mathematics.

Calculator Riddles

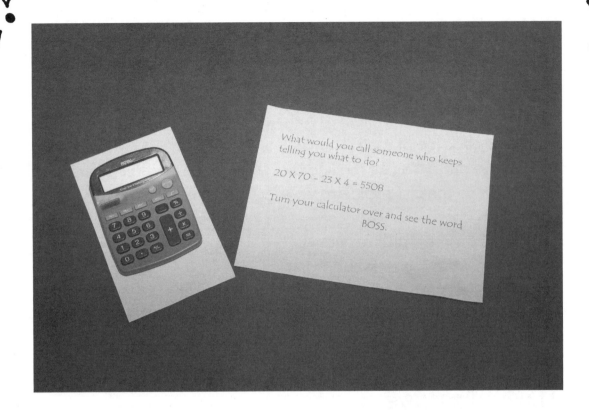

What would you call someone who keeps telling you what to do?

20 X 70 – 23 X 4 = 5508

Turn your calculator over and see the word BOSS.

Materials

1. One calculator
2. Pencil
3. Paper or a journal
4. *Calculator Riddles* by David A. Adler

Extentions

*After students learn how the Calculator Riddles work ask them to create their own riddles for friends to solve.

*Create and bind a class book of riddles and share it with others.

Procedures

1. The calculator has become a very important part of learning math, even for the youngest students. Let's face it: how often do you balance your checkbook without a calculator?

2. Most calculators can be used to write words. By simply turning them upside down, eight of the numbers now look like letters:
   The 8 becomes B.
   The 3 becomes E.
   The 6 becomes G.
   The 4 becomes h.
   The 1 becomes I.
   The 7 becomes L.
   The O becomes O.
   The 5 becomes S.

3. Start by pushing .07734 and turn the calculator over. You have created the word 'hELLO'.

4. Now read some of the riddles from David A. Adler's book along with the given math problem. Allow the students to solve them on their calculators.

Magic Touch

*We like to teach our students how these problems work and then use them as a problem-of-the-day to be added to their math journals.

*Before long, the students will be creating their own riddles for others to solve. This is a great writing and math connection.

NCTM Standards

NUMBERS & OPERATIONS
Standard-The students will understand numbers, ways of representing numbers, relationships among numbers, and number systems.

Standard-The students will understand meanings of operations and how they relate to one another.

Standard-The students will compute fluently and make reasonable estimates.

Candy Bar Fractions

Materials

1. 4 inch x 6 inch piece of tagboard
2. Two page protectors
3. Blackline 6 of candy bar
4. Stapler
5. Glue stick
6. Black fine-tip marker
7. Colored duct tape
8. Brown crayon

Extensions

*Have the students create other candy bar books using different brands of candy bars.

*Have the students write a fraction story to go with a different brand of candy bar.

Procedures

1. Cut both page protectors into quarters. This will give you sixteen pages and you will only use twelve of the pages. The extra pieces can be shared with a friend.

2. Staple all twelve pages inside of the file folder. Cover the staples with duct tape to create a bound edge.

3. On the inside of the back cover, trace around the whole candy bar blackline. Color it brown and draw lines to divide into 12 equal pieces (4 across 3 down). This will represent the whole candy bar.

4. On page one of the book glue the whole candy bar, and on each page following cut away one more piece of the candy bar.

5. Decorate the front cover of the book to look like a real candy bar or use a real candy bar wrapper glued to the front cover.

Magic Touch

*With younger students limit the candy bar pages to show only halves, thirds, or fourths.

*Link this activity to writing by having the students create a poem about their candy bars.

HERSHEY's

NCTM Standard

NUMBER AND OPERATIONS
Standard-The students will understand numbers, ways of representing numbers, relationships among numbers, and number systems.

CONNECTIONS
Standard-The students will recognize and apply mathematics in contexts outside of mathematics.

REPRESENTATION
Standard-The students will create and use representations to organize, record and communicate mathematical ideas.

CD Case Math

Materials

1. Empty CD cases
2. 1/2-inch magnetic strip
3. Magnetic sheets
4. Magnetic metal 4-3/4-inch square
5. Paper
6. Scissors
7. Blackline master 7

Extensions

*Students can create their own math puzzles or find other puzzles that can be placed inside of their CD cases.

*CD cases can also be used to practice spelling, poetry, or vocabulary.

Procedures

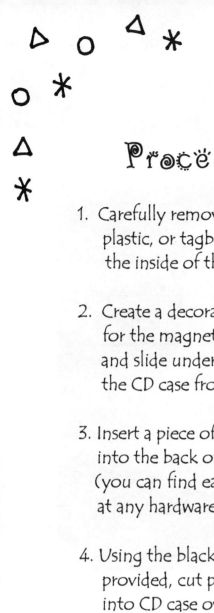

1. Carefully remove any cardboard, plastic, or tagboard from the inside of the case.

2. Create a decorative cover for the magnetic CD case and slide under the tabs for the CD case front cover.

3. Insert a piece of magnetic metal into the back of the CD case (you can find easy-to-cut metal at any hardware store).

4. Using the blackline masters provided, cut puzzle and insert into CD case over metal sheet.

5. Make the numbers and symbols magnetic by attaching magnetic strip to the back and cutting apart.

6. The puzzles can be changed once they have been mastered or taken out and used to practice basic facts.

Magic Touch

*Our students enjoyed making these games so much that they use CD cases for other class projects.

*Send home a note about doing a class project with CD cases and many parents will donate them.

NCTM Standards

NUMBERS AND OPERATIONS
Standard-The students will understand numbers, ways of representing numbers, relationships among numbers, and number systems.

Standard-The students will understand meanings of operations and how they relate to one another.

Standard-The students will compute fluently and make reasonable estimates.

Clocks and Shadows

"Hey You!"

Hey you, do you want to fight?" said The grouchy ladybug.

Meghan

Materials

1. Clocks and Shadows Blackline 8
2. Photograph of person showing an action
3. Glue
4. Crayons, colored pencils, or markers

Extensions

*Use Eric Carle's book *The Grouchy Ladybug.* Compare the location of the sun and the time in the story to the sun and time where you live.

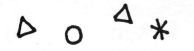

Procedures

1. Take a photograph of someone. (Showing an action helps create an interesting picture.)

2. Cut away the background from the person's body.

3. Glue the photograph cut out to the Clock and Shadow blackline master 8.

4. Create a background around the photograph that matches the action in the photo. Example: If the photo is of someone at bat then draw a baseball field around him/her.

5. With a black marker, draw a shadow to the photograph and the sun in the sky. The shadow should be in correct alignment to the sun.

6. With a black markers, add clock hands to show the time of day illustrated in the picture.

7. Finally, sequence student's pictures by the time of day on the clocks.

Magic Touch

*Have each student write a story about their action illustration. They should include a description of the time of day. Students can also take a series of pictures during a day, illustrating them all in the same way, and sequencing the story by events.

NCTM Standard

COMMUNICATION
Standard-The students will organize and consolidate their mathematical thinking through communication.

Standard-The students will communicate their mathematical thinking coherently and clearly to peers, teachers, and others.

CONNECTIONS
Standard-The students will recognize the connections among mathematical ideas.

Coin Time Lines

Materials

1. Copies of Timeline blackline master 9, one for each year
2. A coin with the date to match each year on the timeline
3. Scissors
4. Scotch tape or glue
5. Crayons, colored pencils, or markers

Extensions

*Have the students add a photograph to each page of their timelines.
*The students also can write a story about their lives using the timeline as an outline to structure the story.

Procedures

1. Begin by having the students search for coins, one for each year on their timeline.

2. Have the students fill in each year of their timeline with the number of the year, their age during that year, a coin to represent that year, and at least three events that occurred in their life during that year. (Younger students can use illustrations on their timeline in place of words.)

3. Once all years of their timeline have been completed, cut apart each year of their timeline, and glue or tape them in order.

4. Have the students share some of the major events on their timeline as an oral presentation or display for others to read.

NOTE-You may only want to do a selected number of years for a timeline with older students since this could become a lengthy project with older students.

Magic Touch

*This project can be extended by having the student's think about their future. Have them draw or paint a picture of how they will look in the future (10-20 years). Extend this project by assigning a narrative essay about what they hope their lives will be like at that time.

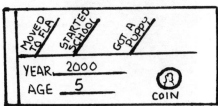

NCTM Standards

COMMUNICATION
Standard-The students will organize and consolidate their mathematical thinking through communication.

Standard-The students will communicate their mathematical thinking coherently and clearly to peers, teachers, and others.

CONNECTIONS
Standard-The students will recognize and apply mathematics in contexts outside of mathematics.

Counting Rhyme Books

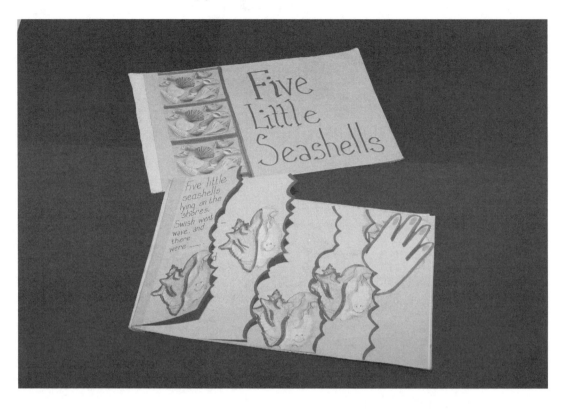

Materials

1. Three sheets of paper
   (8-1/2-inches by 11-inches)
   or use blackline master 10
2. Stapler
3. Crayons, colored pencils,
   or markers

Extensions

*This style of book can
be used in other subject
areas to create study
sheets, vocabulary packets,
or research projects.

Procedures

1. Stack the three sheets of paper so the top of each page is one inch down from the last one. (See Blackline master 10)

2. Flip the pages over so varied lengths are showing along the bottom.

3. Fold top forward so you see six levels of paper. Now your book should have six pages, each a different length.

4. Staple three times through all layers of paper along the folded edge.

5. Label or illustrate each flap to go along with your theme.

6. Now you are ready to open each flap and fill in the appropriate information.

7. Use a counting poem as your words for your book. Our favorite is *Five Little Seashells*. We make the pages from blue paper and add a seashell to each page. Each page turned washes away a shell.

Magic Touch

*The Bag Ladies like to add some extra touches like real sand or glitter to each page. If you live near the beach, you can also collect shells to glue on each page.

*The teacher also can make a Big Book while the students make individual books.

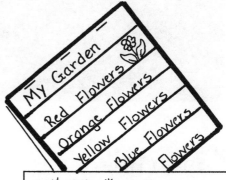

NCTM Standard

NUMBERS AND OPERATIONS
Standard-The students will understand numbers, ways of representing numbers, relationships among numbers, and number systems.

Standard-The students will understand the meanings of operations and how they relate to one another.

COMMUNICATION
Standard-The students will use the language of mathematics to express mathematical ideas precisely.

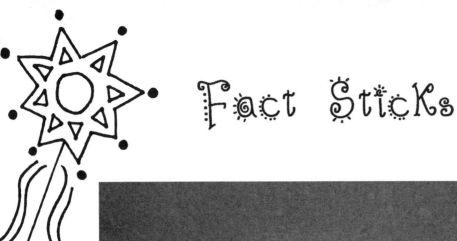

Fact Sticks

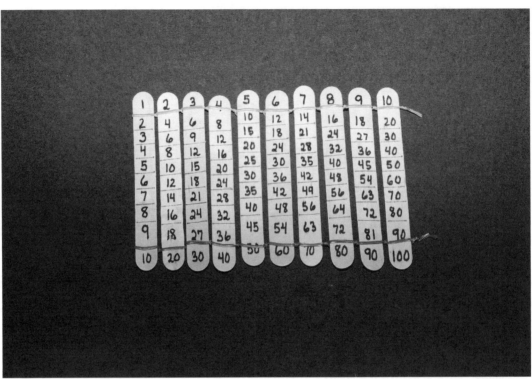

Materials

1. Ten wooden tongue depressor sticks
2. Four feet of lacing material (one of the following: wire tie, ribbon, yarn, or plastic lacing string.)
3. Black fine-tip marker
4. Scissors

Extensions

*Students can attach their fact sticks inside of a loose-leaf notebook for safe-keeping.

*Students can work in teams to create different fact families or sets of facts.

Procedures

1. Cut the four-foot long piece of lacing into two equal pieces.

2. Begin with one stick, and fold lacing material in half, twisting around stick at one end. Repeat the same process with the other piece of lacing at the other end of the stick.

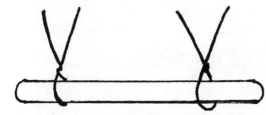

3. Add another stick and repeat Step 2. Continue this process until all sticks are added.

4. Use each stick to write a fact, or create a complete multiplication table on the set of sticks.

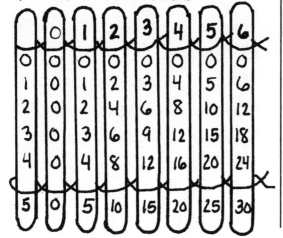

Magic Touch

*The Bag Ladies have found that when students create projects, they truly learn and understand a concept, and they remember the concept for a longer period of time.

*If your students enjoyed this this activity, try making our Napier Bones with them, too.

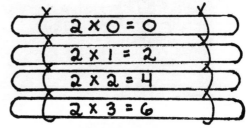

2 X 0 = 0
2 X 1 = 2
2 X 2 = 4
2 X 3 = 6

NCTM Standards

NUMBERS AND OPERATIONS
Standard–The students will understand numbers, ways of representing numbers, relationships among numbers, and number systems.

Standard–The students will understand meanings of operations and how they relate to one another.

Standard–The students will compute fluently and make reasonable estimates.

Folder Frame Problems

Materials

1. One-half of a file folder, cut horizontally
2. One page protector cut in half horizontally
3. 4-1/4-inch by 7-1/2 inch sheet of white paper
4. Ruler
5. Scissors
6. Crayons, colored pencils or markers

Extensions

*The file folder frames also can be used to frame other types of student work and made in a variety of sizes.

*Add two magnetic sticker dots to the back of the folder frame so it can be hung on a magnetic surface.

Procedures

1. Trim edge of the folder to remove tab. If an uneven edge remains flip to the back side.

2. Using a ruler, measure approximately one inch in on the front side of the file folder to make a border. Cut out the center section of the folder front to make a frame.

3. Center the sheet of white paper inside of the folder frame and draw lines to mark the edges of the frame. Then remove paper from the frame.

4. Decorate your frame with math symbols. Create an illustration and write a problem to match it.

5. Slide your math problem into the page protector, center it inside of the frame, and tape in place.

6. Tape the folder frame closed with Scotch tape and display your problem.

Magic Touch

*Have the students use their small folder frames as rough drafts. Once the frames have been revised and edited, have them create larger versions of the picture and problem. These can be displayed as an art exhibit. Invite others to try solving your "artistic problems."

NCTM Standards

PROBLEM SOLVING
Standard–The students will build new mathematical knowledge through problem solving.

Standard–The students will solve problems that arise in mathematics and in other contexts.

Standard–The students will apply and adapt a variety of appropriate strategies to solve problems.

Geometry Quilts

Materials

1. Sticky-back Fun Foam
2. Stamp pads of various colors
3. Blackline master 11, quilt squares, and quilt patterns
4. Scissors
5. 2-inch by 2-inch wooden blocks, one for each shape in quilt design

Extensions

*Assemble and display all of the quilt squares that your students created to make a class quilt.

*Have the students create their own designs for quilt squares, researching to see if any similar designs already exist.

Procedures

1. Cut sticky-back Fun Foam into desired shapes for your quilt pattern.

2. Peel paper from the sticky side of the Fun Foam and attach each shape to a wooden block.

3. Your shapes are now ready to be used as rubber stamps.

4. Use your shape stamps to create a pattern on the Quilt Square blackline 11.

HINT-Refer to the Quilt Pattern sample sheet for ideas on quilt designs and patterns.

*Precut geometric stamping blocks can be purchased from:
A Small Woodworking Company
Jim & Kathy Biogett
PO Box 460
34207 82nd Ave. So.
Roy, WA 98680
(206) 458-3370

Magic Touch

*Invite a quilter into your classroom to speak about the art of quilting.

*Have a class quilting bee and create a fabric quilt. Have each student create a different type of quilt square. Follow the quilting bee with a quilt show for other classes and parents.

NCTM Standards

GEOMETRY
Standard-The students will apply transformations and use symmetry to analyze mathematical situation.

Standard-The students will use visualization, spatial reasoning, and geometric modeling to solve problems.

Standard-The students will specify locations and describe spatial relationships using coordinate geometry and other representational systems.

Googol Necklace

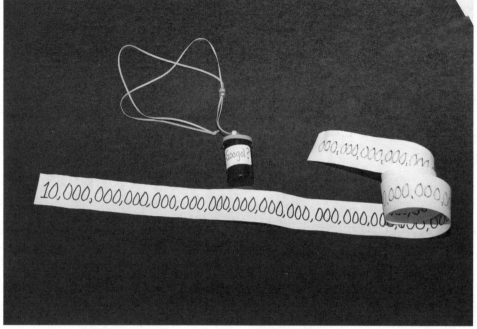

Materials

1. Small recycled jar or bottle
   Examples: film container or
   small spice jar
2. 32-inch to 36-inch length
   plastic lacing cord
3. One to three pony beads
4. One screw with a looped eye
5. Adding machine tape cut to fit
   inside of container
6. Scissors
7. Black permanent marker

Extensions

*This style of necklace also
can be used to hold other
activities such as Bug Bean
Counters, poems, or plant
starters.

*The students can come up
with other uses for their
Googol Necklaces or
exchange them with friends.

Procedures

1. Wash jar or container, remove label, and dry thoroughly. Carefully poke the screw with the looped eye through the lid of the container.

2. Thread the end of the lacing through the looped eye and string pony beads through both ends of lacing. Now tie the lacing ends into a knot.

3. Using a permanent marker, decorate the outside of your container with the word "Googol" or a question about what a Googol might be.

4. Complete your necklace by writing the number One Googol on the adding machine tape and enclosing it inside of the container.

(In case you don't know what a Googol is, it is a 1 followed by 100 zeros. A Googol is a real number. It was given that name by the nine-year-old nephew of Dr. Edward Kasner in the late 1930s and has been called a googol ever since.)

Magic Touch

*Purchase a variety of beads and colors of lacing, and allow the students some creative leeway as they assemble their necklaces.

*Clear film containers make great plant-starter necklaces. Place a damp piece of cotton and a few seeds inside.

SEED STARTER

NCTM Standard

NUMBER AND OPERATIONS
Standard-The students will understand numbers, ways of representing numbers, relationships among numbers, and number systems.

COMMUNICATION
Standard-The students will communicate their mathematical thinking coherently and clearly to peers, teachers, and others.

CONNECTIONS
Standard-The students will recognize and use connections among mathematical ideas.

Hefty Plate Math

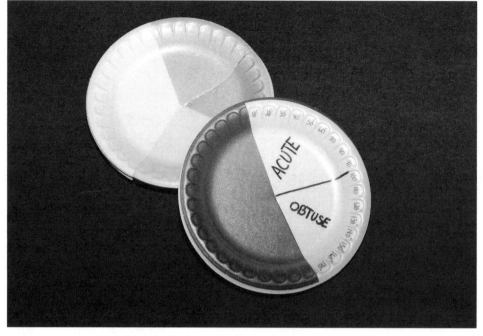

Materials

1. Two to four different colors of Hefty-brand styrofoam plates.
2. Scissors

*Hefty-brand styrofoam plates work best because they have 36 thumbprints around the edge, representing 10 degrees of a each 360-degree circle.

Extensions

*Measurements of an angle
*Compare and make models of halves, thirds, and fourths.
*Show different times using the plates as a clock face.
*Make a 2-3-4 color spinner to discuss probability.
*Use plates for sorting.

Procedures

TWO PLATES

1. Cut from one edge of each plate to the center on both plates.

2. Slide one plate through the other at the slit until the centers meet. Turn one plate to show both colors.

THREE PLATES

1. Cut from one edge of each plate to the center on both plates.

2. Stack two plates together and line up their slits. Slide the stacked plates through the other plate until the centers meet. Turn two plates to show all three colors.

FOUR PLATES

1. Cut from one edge of each plate to the center on both plates.

2. Stack two plates together on each side and line up their slits. Slide the plates together through the other plates at the slits until the centers meet. Turn three plates to show all colors show and create a circle graph.

Magic Touch

*Teach younger students the basics of circle graphing by giving them 36 objects that can be sorted into four categories. Have them turn the plate 10 degrees or one thumbprint for each of the 36 objects. Example: If they have four blue objects, turn the plate to show four blue thumbprints. Ask them to write sentences to compare the groups on their graph.

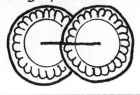

NCTM Standard

DATA AND PROBABILITY
Standard-The students will select and use appropriate statistical methods to analyze data.

Standard-The students will develop and evaluate inferences and predictions that are based on data.

Standard-The students will understand and apply basic concepts of probability.

Hundred Penny Boxes

Materials

1. Greeting cards
   in a variety of sizes
2. 100 pennies
3. Scissors
4. Tape

Extensions

*Create boxes for younger
 students to put their teeth
 in when lost.
*Create a set of boxes that
 fit inside of each other.
*Create boxes to hold
 student-made gifts.

Procedures

1. Cut a greeting card along fold and separate front of card from the inside.
2. Using message piece of the card only cut away ¼-inch from the length and width.
3. Start by folding the inside piece of card first. Fold message piece of card in half lengthwise and unfold.
4. Fold each lengthwise side of the card to the center fold line. We call this a double-door fold.

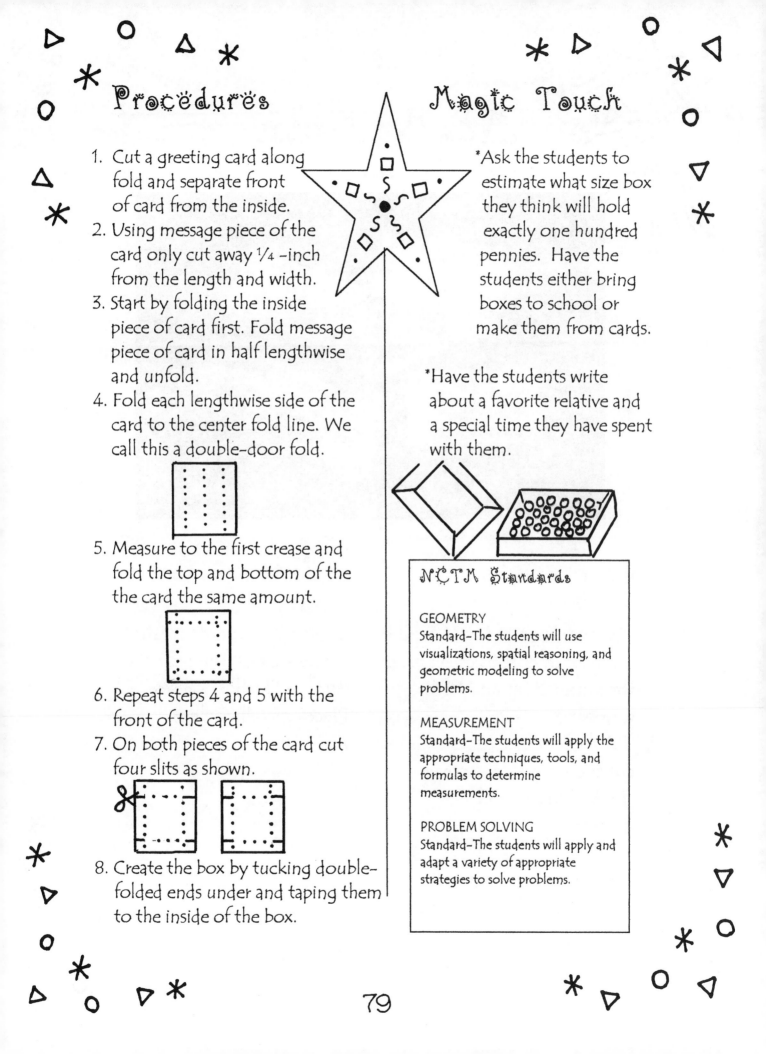

5. Measure to the first crease and fold the top and bottom of the the card the same amount.

6. Repeat steps 4 and 5 with the front of the card.
7. On both pieces of the card cut four slits as shown.

8. Create the box by tucking double-folded ends under and taping them to the inside of the box.

Magic Touch

*Ask the students to estimate what size box they think will hold exactly one hundred pennies. Have the students either bring boxes to school or make them from cards.

*Have the students write about a favorite relative and a special time they have spent with them.

NCTM Standards

GEOMETRY
Standard-The students will use visualizations, spatial reasoning, and geometric modeling to solve problems.

MEASUREMENT
Standard-The students will apply the appropriate techniques, tools, and formulas to determine measurements.

PROBLEM SOLVING
Standard-The students will apply and adapt a variety of appropriate strategies to solve problems.

M&M Math

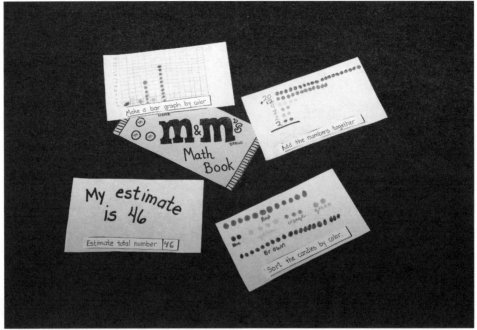

Materials

1. One package of M&M candies
2. A sheet of construction paper the same size as an M&M wrapper.
3. 20 sheets white paper cut the same size as cover
4. Metal binding rings
5. Scissors
6. Glue
7. Tempera paint and markers
8. M&M Blackline master 12

Extensions

*Have the students create other stories using candy, such as Skittles, Reeses Pieces or Jelly Bellies.

Procedures

1. Have the students cut apart each strip of words and glue to each page of their books.

2. The students should trace over the words with markers and use the words as a guide for their illustrations.

3. To illustrate the M&Ms, the students can dip their pinky fingers into the tempera paint and dab it on their paper to look like M&M candies.

4. Allow paint to dry, hole punch each page, and bind with metal rings.

5. The students can create their own covers with markers and tempera paint, or they can carefully open the package of M&Ms and glue to the front.

Magic Touch

*The students can practice the steps in their M&M story with real M&Ms and munch along the way.

*The students could also continue the story with their own sets of problems that go with their package of candies.

NCTM Standard

DATA AND PROBABILITY
Standard-The students will formulate questions that can be addressed with data and collect, organize, and display data to answer them.

Standard-The students will select and use appropriate statistical methods to analyze data.

Standard-The students will understand and apply basic concepts of probability.

Make your own Tangrams

Materials

1. 3-inch by 3-inch square Fun Foam
2. Copy of Tangram Blackline 13
3. Scissors
4. Zipper-style baggie to store tangrams.

Extensions

*Share the story, *The Tortoise Who Bragged* adapted by Betsy Franco. This story is told using trigrams, a set of nine pieces that are all right triangles. This story usually comes with a set of trigrams.

Procedures

1. Fold the Fun Foam square at a diagonal and cut along the fold line. (We call this a taco-shell fold.)

2. Set one of these triangles aside. Cut the other one in half. Set these two triangles aside.

3. Using the large triangle from above, fold the top point of the triangle to meet the lower edge. Cut along this folded line.

4. Now fold the trapezoid in half symmetrically and cut on the fold. Set one half of the trapezoid aside. Fold one piece so the pointed edge meets the opposite side, and cut.

5. Fold the remaining trapezoid as illustrated below to create a parallelogram and a triangle.

6. Store your tangrams in zipper-style baggies.

Magic Touch

*Have the students practice creating different characters and objects using their shapes. Choose some of their favorites and create a story with them. First, have them plan the tans they will use and practice making each tangram puzzles. Use the provided blackline as a planning sheet for their stories.

NCTM Standards

GEOMETRY
Standard-The students will specify locations and describe spatial relationships using co-ordinate geometry and other representational systems.

Standard-The students will apply transformations and use symmetry to analyze mathematical situations.

Standard-The students will use visualization, spatial reasoning, and geometric modeling to solve problems.

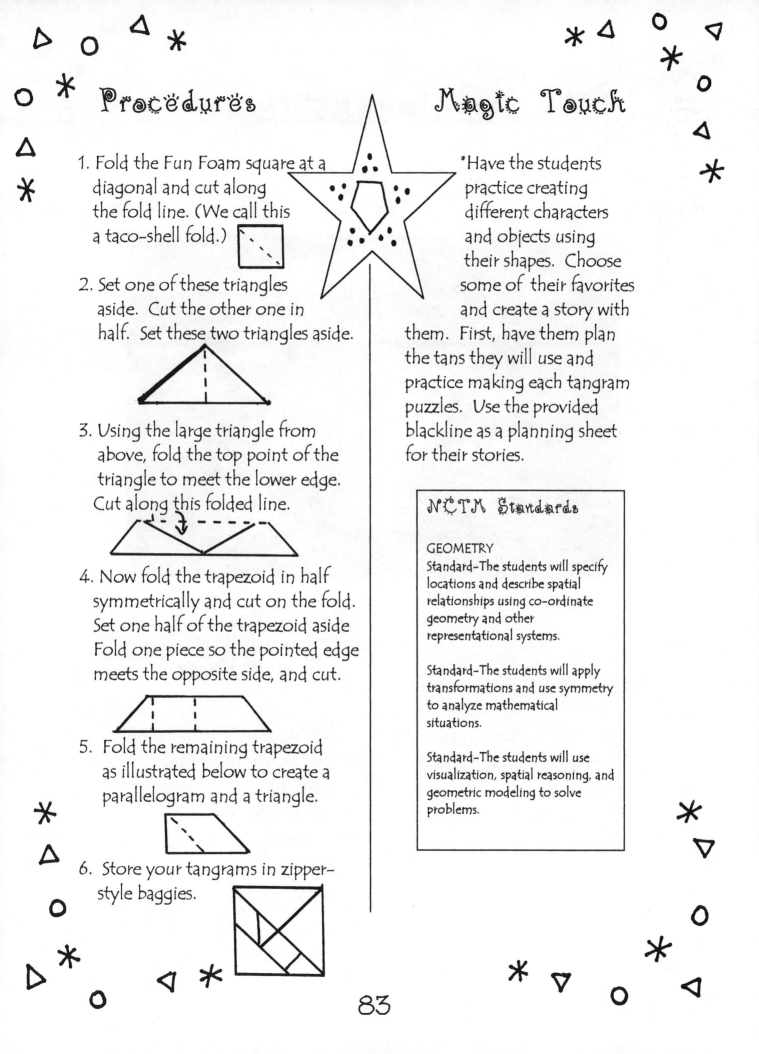

Manipulative Manager

Materials

1. Four brown paper lunch bags
2. Clear-wide packaging tape
3. Scissors
4. Fine-tip black marker

Extensions

*The Manipulative Manager also can be made in a larger size using a regular size grocery bag.

*The Manipulative Manager can be used to store other things, spelling lists, vocabulary flashcards, or a study guide organizer.

Procedures

1. Cut the bottom off of each bag.

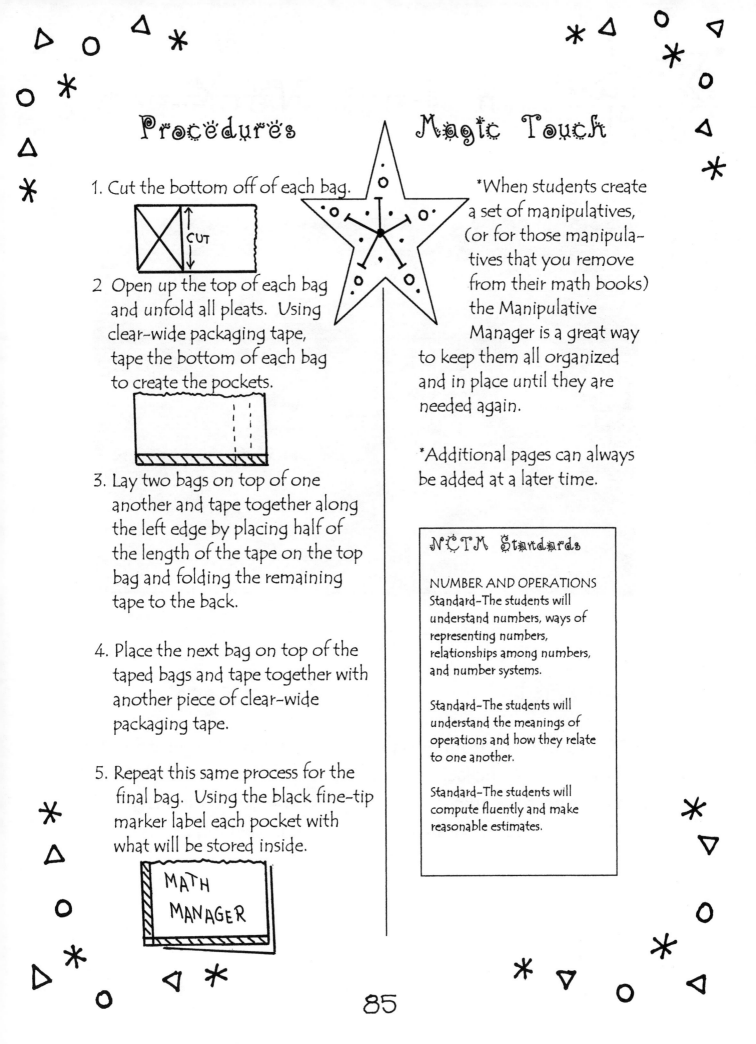

CUT

2. Open up the top of each bag and unfold all pleats. Using clear-wide packaging tape, tape the bottom of each bag to create the pockets.

3. Lay two bags on top of one another and tape together along the left edge by placing half of the length of the tape on the top bag and folding the remaining tape to the back.

4. Place the next bag on top of the taped bags and tape together with another piece of clear-wide packaging tape.

5. Repeat this same process for the final bag. Using the black fine-tip marker label each pocket with what will be stored inside.

MATH MANAGER

Magic Touch

*When students create a set of manipulatives, (or for those manipulatives that you remove from their math books) the Manipulative Manager is a great way to keep them all organized and in place until they are needed again.

*Additional pages can always be added at a later time.

NCTM Standards

NUMBER AND OPERATIONS
Standard-The students will understand numbers, ways of representing numbers, relationships among numbers, and number systems.

Standard-The students will understand the meanings of operations and how they relate to one another.

Standard-The students will compute fluently and make reasonable estimates.

Math Fact Necklace

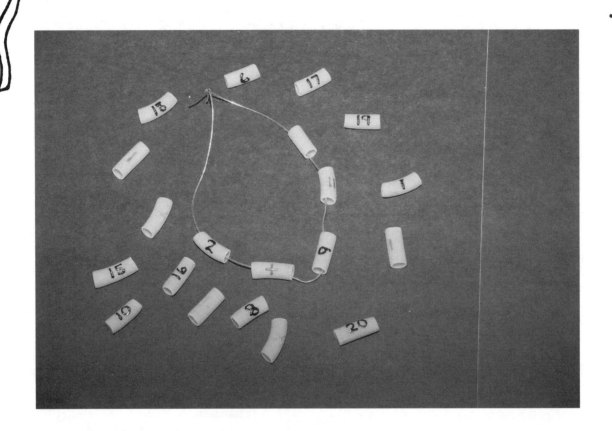

Materials

1. 25 uncooked rigatoni noodles
2. Two feet of plastic lacing
3. Black fine-tip marker
4. Math basic fact flashcards
5. Zipper-style baggies for storage

Extensions

*This activity can be done with letters for students to practice, vocabulary words, spelling words or language skills.

Procedures

1. Using the black fine-tip marker, have students write the numbers 0 through 9, one number on each piece of rigatoni. Repeat Step One so you have two rigatoni with the same number. This will allow them to practice doubles (4+4=) fact problems.

2. With the remaining rigatoni, write the math signs (+,-, X, ÷, =) one to a rigatoni noodle. If you have extra you can make extras of any of the signs.

3. The students now can use their rigatoni to create math sentences by stringing the noodles onto the plastic lacing cord.

4. When the students are finished practicing their math facts they can wear a math fact sentence on their necklace. Place the extra rigatoni in the zipper-style baggie, and they are ready to use on another day.

Magic Touch

*Before writing the numbers and math signs on the rigatoni, try dying the rigatoni noodles with rubbing alcohol tinted with food coloring. Once the noodles have taken on the color of the alcohol, remove from liquid and allow to dry completely on a paper towel. Once the noodles are dry, write the numbers with the fine-tip marker.

NCTM Standards

NUMBER AND OPERATIONS
Standard-The students will understand numbers, ways of representing numbers, relationships among numbers, and number systems.

Standard-The students will understand the meanings of operations and how they relate to one another.

Standard-The students will compute fluently and make reasonable estimates.

Math Wallets

Materials

1. Wallet Blackline master 14
2. Scissors
3. Scotch tape
4. Crayons, colored pencils, or markers

Extensions

*Have the students design their own money and explain why they used the colors, pictures, and numbers that they choose.

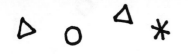

Procedures

Magic Touch

1. Cut out the blackline master on the solid black lines.

2. Use the Scotch tape to tape the ends of the wallet closed to secure.

   TAPE →

3. Create drawings and written information to match the story that was read.

4. Create money to go inside the wallet that complements the story.

Suggestions

It is best to use a story that deals with money and then incorporate it into a math lesson.

The money that the students create can be used to create board games and learning centers.

This activity also can include teaching students about writing checks, ATM cards and credit cards. Have them create their own and add them to their wallets.

*Have the students first create a wallet from paper as a rough draft. Then reproduce it on a piece of vinyl fabric and stitch it closed with plastic lacing cord to look like a real wallet.

*Ask students to bring in an old wallet from home (after asking mom or dad) then fill the wallet with details from the story.

NCTM Standards

REPRESENTATION
Standard-The students will create and use representations to organize, record, and communicate mathematical ideas.

Standard-The students will select, apply, and translate among mathematical representations to solve problems.

Standard-The students will use representations to model and interpret physical, social, mathematical phenomena.

My Math Dream

Materials

1. Blackline master 15
   My Math Dream
2. Crayons, colored pencils
   or markers
3. *Amanda Bean's Amazing Dream*
   by Cindy Neuschwander

Extensions

*After reading the story,
revisit the illustrations and
discuss with the student
the different ways objects
can be counted. This also
can be done with other
picture books.

Procedures

Magic Touch

1. After reading the story *Amanda Bean's Amazing Dream* discuss things that would be difficult to count by ones.

2. The teacher and students could list these things on chart paper to give students ideas for illustrations.

3. Give each student a copy of the blackline master and ask them to create an illustration of something with a large number that they could use multiplication to count.

4. Share some completed illustrations with the class and match a multiplication sentence to each illustration.

5. Expand this activity by having the students create their own versions of *Amanda Bean's Amazing Dream* but change the title to *(Student's Name)'s Amazing Dream.*

*Student's stories can be illustrated and published at a classroom publishing center. This would be a great opportunity for the students to learn to bind their own books. Be sure to allow some time for the students to share their stories.

Name Game

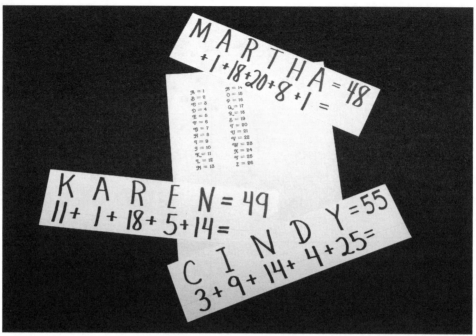

Materials

1. Paper
2. Pencil
3. Calculator

Extensions

*Have the students create sentences with different point values. Can you create a sentence worth 200 points?

*Reverse the values of each letter and see if it makes a difference in the value of your name.
A-26, B-25, C-24 to Z-1

Magic Touch

1. In mathematics letters can sometimes be used to represent numbers. This type of math is called algebra. It is a useful way of doing math when you are not sure what numbers should be used.

2. Create a code for the letters of the alphabet, a=1, b=2, c=3, d=4, until you get to z=26.

3. Once you have given a value to each letter of the alphabet figure out what your first name is worth.

   Cindy is worth 55 points because C=3, I=9, N=14, D=4, Y=25
   3 + 9 + 14 + 4 + 25 = 55

4. Now try this with your middle and last name. Compare names of friends to your name and see who's name is worth the most. Maybe you even have a "twin", someone else with a name that has the same numerical value as yours.

*Give each child a sentence strip. Ask students to display their full names and the values for each letter. Create a class graph showing the value of everyone's name. Discuss and compare the information that was put on the graph.

NCTM Standards

ALGEBRA
Standard-The students will understand patterns, relations, and functions.

Standard-The students will represent and analyze mathematical situations and structures using algebraic symbols.

Standard-The students will use mathematical models to represent and understand quantitative relationships.

Standard-The students will analyze changes in various contexts.

Napier Bones

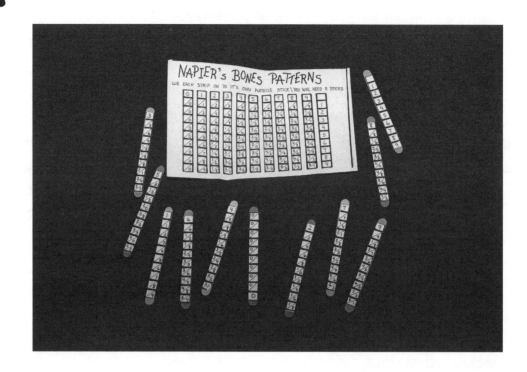

NAPIER'S BONES PATTERNS
USE EACH STRIP ON TO IT'S OWN POPSICLE STICK \ YOU WILL NEED 11 STICKS

Materials

1. Eleven popsicle sticks
2. Glue
3 Scissors
4. Zipper-style baggie to store Napier Bones
5. Napier Bone Blackline 17

Extensions

*Have the students create a story that involves using Napier Bones to solve the problems.

*Have a contest to see how quickly students can solve math problems using their Napier Bones.

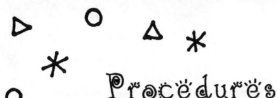

Magic Touch

1. Cut out the eleven strips on the blackline master 17. Glue each strip to a popsicle stick.

2. You are now ready to use your Napier Bones to multiply.

What are Napier Bones?

Napier Bones are ten sticks that help you multiply long numbers quickly. A set of multiples is written on each stick and then added to determine the answer to a problem.

EXAMPLE: 432 X 4 = ___

1. Put stick 2 in the one's column, stick 3 in the ten's column, and stick 4 in the hundred's column.

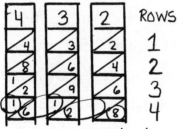

2. Since you are multiplying by 4, move along row 4, from right to left and add together the numbers in each diagonal column.

*Buy the colored popsicle sticks to make Napier Bones seem extra-special.

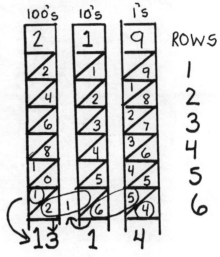

219 x 6 = 1314

Number Stamps

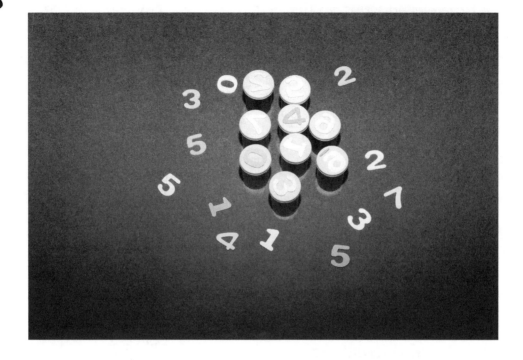

Materials

1. Fun Foam pre-cut numbers (found at any craft store)
2. Empty 35mm film containers, one for each number stamp
4. Glue
5. Stamp pads
6. Paper

Extensions

*Have the students create their own math equation stories and use their rubber stamps to show their math problems. Example: Two rabbits were in the garden. It took the first rabbit five hops to get to the carrots. It took the second rabbit three more hops than the first. How many hops did the second rabbit take?

Procedures

1. Each film container will make one rubber stamp. Select one fun foam number from package 0-9.

2. Using a extra-strong holding glue, glue one foam number to the lid of each film container. Remember to glue them on backwards so they print correctly.

3. Allow glue to dry completely before you use these as rubber stamps.

4. Once the glue is dry, your rubber stamps are ready to use. Gently touch the fun foam number to the stamp pad and press onto paper.

5. Use your rubber stamps to create math problems, answer by stamping the answers.

6. These rubber stamps can make practicing the basic facts fun. Instead of just saying the answer, students can stamp the answer and hold it up.

Magic Touch

*Have the students make rubber stamps for the math symbols. To make the symbols you will need to purchase a sheet of Fun Foam and cut shapes out and glue to each film container.

*You also can substitute water-based markers for the stamp pads. Just color the number on the bottom of the stamp with the marker and then press onto paper.

NCTM Standards

NUMBER & OPERATIONS
Standard-The students will understand numbers, ways of representing numbers, relationships among numbers, and number systems.

Standard-The students will compute fluently and make reasonable estimates.

Origami Book

Can you cross each bridge once and only once, without swimming, jumping, boating, or flying across the river.

Materials

1. Two 6-inch squares of an old road map
2. One 12-inch piece of thin craft ribbon
3. Two squares of tagboard 4-inches by 4-inches
4. One square of white paper 8-inches by 8-inches
5. Scotch tape & glue stick
6. Scissors

Extensions

*Additional pages can be added to this book by repeating Steps 3 to 5 with additional sheets of paper. Glue squares together, then glue top square to the front cover and last square to the back cover.

Procedures

1. Front & back cover directions: Lay map squares in front of you in a diamond position, a point facing you. Rub glue stick around tagboard and fold map down. Repeat step 1 with the other piece of tagboard and map.

GLUE AND FOLD

2. Place both cover pieces, right side down, on a table with two of their corners about ¼ inch apart. Lay ribbon across tagboard evenly and tape down to secure in place. Set aside.

3. Inside page directions: Using the 8-inch by 8-inch square of paper, fold once vertically (hot dog fold), then once horizontally (hamburger fold) and open.

4. Now fold diagonally (taco fold), open taco fold, and fold on the same diagonal line but in the opposite direction. This will make the paper easier to work with for the next step.

5. Hold the paper at the top of the taco fold and tuck triangles inside the squares.

6. Glue one side of the paper square to the inside of the front cover and one side to the back cover. You are now ready to create a bridge problem inside.

7. Read the Letter K page in *G is for Googol* to learn more about bridge problems.

Magic Touch

*Create a map of a town that is an island and has more than one bridge. The map should show a river and land on the outside, an island in the middle, and four or more bridges. Share the maze with friend and tell them they can cross each bridge once and only once, without jumping, swimming, boating or flying to cross.

99

Paper Clip Circumference

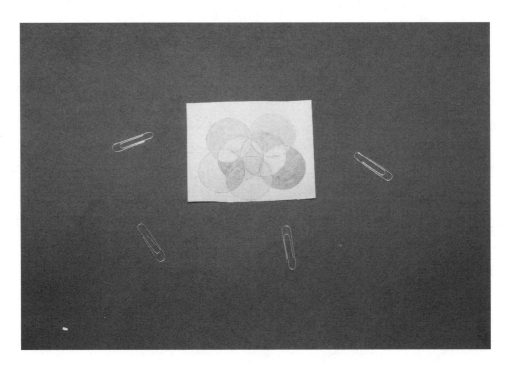

Materials

1. One 8-1/2-inch by 11-inch sheet of paper
2. A variety of sizes of paper clips
3. Two pencils or pens
4. Crayons, colored pencils, or markers

Extensions

*Try drawing different patterns. First draw a circle, then place one of the pencils and paper clip on the edge of the circle and draw another circle. Continue until you have created a pattern.

Procedures

1. You can make a beautiful flower shape by making circles, and you don't even need a compass.

2. Draw a circle in the middle of your paper by placing one pencil over the end of the paper clip. Now place the other pencil in the other end of the paper clip.

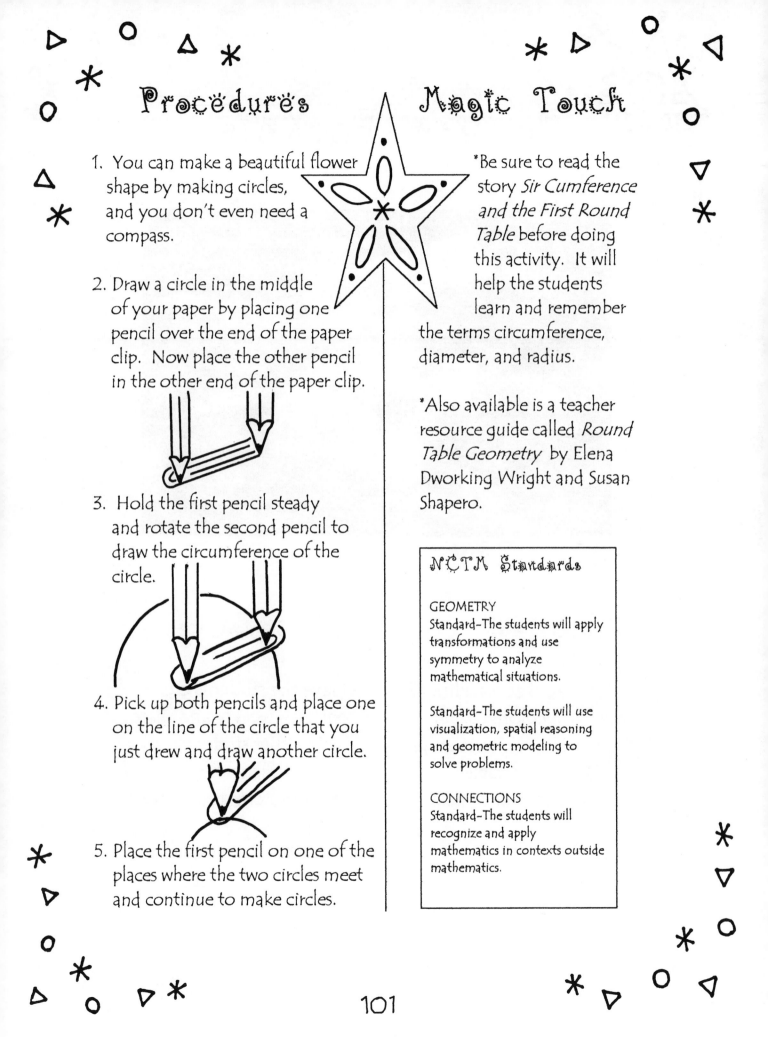

3. Hold the first pencil steady and rotate the second pencil to draw the circumference of the circle.

4. Pick up both pencils and place one on the line of the circle that you just drew and draw another circle.

5. Place the first pencil on one of the places where the two circles meet and continue to make circles.

Magic Touch

*Be sure to read the story *Sir Cumference and the First Round Table* before doing this activity. It will help the students learn and remember the terms circumference, diameter, and radius.

*Also available is a teacher resource guide called *Round Table Geometry* by Elena Dworking Wright and Susan Shapero.

NCTM Standards

GEOMETRY
Standard-The students will apply transformations and use symmetry to analyze mathematical situations.

Standard-The students will use visualization, spatial reasoning and geometric modeling to solve problems.

CONNECTIONS
Standard-The students will recognize and apply mathematics in contexts outside mathematics.

Pattern Pockets

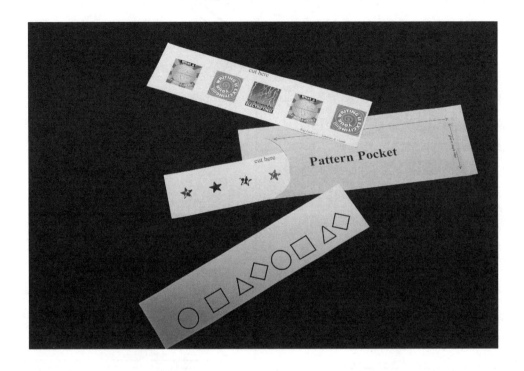

Materials

1. Pattern Pocket Blackline 17 copied on colored paper
2. One or two sentence strips
3. Scotch tape or stapler
4. Crayons, colored pencils or markers
5. Scissors
6. Stickers

Extensions

*Have the students create patterns weekly and share with other students.

*Have students rename their pattern using letters or numbers
EXAMPLE: A-B-A-B-A-B
A-A-B-A-A-B
A-B-C-A-B-C

Procedures

1. Cut on the curved dotted line to create an opening in the end of the Pattern Pocket.

2. Fold the Pattern Pocket on the center fold line.

   PATTERN POCKET ← FOLD

3. Tape or staple the Pattern Pocket around the uncut edges.

4. For individual, group, or teacher-directed projects, draw a pattern on the sentence strip with crayons, colored pencils, or markers.

5. Insert the sentence strip into the Pattern Pocket.

6. Pull the sentence strip out of the pocket one symbol at a time.

7. Ask the students to try to predict what will come next in the pattern.

HINT-Try this as a teacher-directed activity, then allow students to create their own patterns for the Pocket Pockets.

Magic Touch

*Using the book *Picture Pie* by Ed Emberly have the students use the characters and shapes as part of their patterns.

*Have the students create a story about the characters on their pattern strips.

NCTM Standards

ALGEBRA
Standard-The students will understand patterns, relations, and functions.

Standard-The students will represent and analyze mathematical situations and structures using algebraic symbols.

REPRESENTATIONS
Standard-The students will create and use representations to organize, record, and communicate mathematical ideas.

Percent Grids

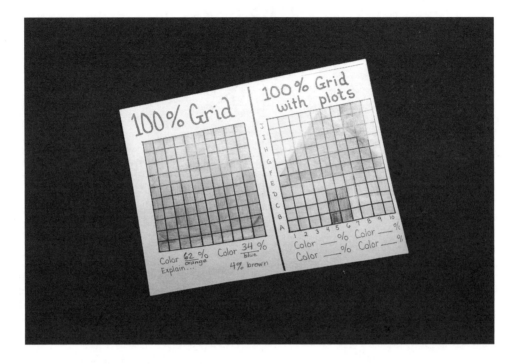

Materials

1. A copy of 100-square Blackline master 18
2. Crayons, colored pencils or markers

<u>Optional materials</u>
1. Construction paper cut into small squares
2. Glue

Extensions

*Using optional materials, create pictures by gluing small squares of construction paper in the boxes instead of coloring.

*Create a picture using the grid paper and have the students create plot points and then color. Example: color A1-green, A2-red.

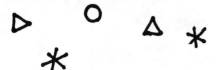

Procedures

Magic Touch

1. Have the students create a picture using exactly half of the one hundred squares.

2. They will use two different colors; one to create the object and the other to create the background.

HINT-To color half of the hundred squares you must color 50 small squares. When you plan your design mark the squares lightly with a pencil to make changes easier.

*As students continue this project have them try different percentages of color to create their pictures.
EXAMPLE:

    30% color 1, 70% color 2

        or

    Use 4 colors, 25% of each color. When the students finish they can ask a friend to identify the percentages of each color they used to create a picture.

*Design a Magic Carpet use six colors and a one hundred square grid to create a carpet design. Their design could include, 50% blue, 10% red, 10% yellow, 10% white, 10% black, and 10% green. Look at catalogs to get some ideas for rug designs.

NCTM Standards

DATA ANALYSIS AND PROBABILITY
Standard-The students will formulate questions that can be addressed with data and collect, organize, and display relevant data to answer them.

Standard-The students will select and use appropriate statistical methods to analyze data.

Spaghetti Lines

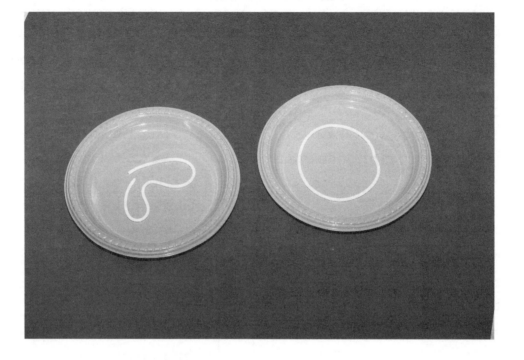

Materials

1. A few pieces of uncooked spaghetti
2. A few pieces of cooked spaghetti
3. One plastic or paper plate

Extensions

*This same activity using both cooked and uncooked spaghetti can be done to write words or numbers.

Procedures

1. Provide each student with some uncooked spaghetti, explaining that each piece of spaghetti represents a line segment. Have them compare this line segment to a shape and discuss how they are the same and different.

2. Provide each student with some cooked spaghetti on a paper or plastic plate. Have the students begin by making lines with the spaghetti pieces, some that curve like the letter S and other lines that are straight.

3. If the students understand these concepts, have them continue by creating opened and closed figures using their cooked spaghetti.

4. They can also create different geometric shapes and discuss sides and corners.

5. The students can continue this activity by writing, about the shapes they have created or illustrating them on drawing paper.

Magic Touch

*This activity works well with *The Straight Line Wonder* by Mem Fox. The students can manipulate the cooked spaghetti into opened and closed figures as you read the story. It is helpful if you demonstrate the position of the lines on the overhead as the students work at their desks.

NCTM Standards

GEOMETRY
Standard–The students will analyze characteristics and properties of two- and three-dimensional geometric shapes and develop mathematical arguments about geometric relationships.

Standard–The students will apply transformations and use symmetry to analyze mathematical situations.

Standard–The students will use visualization, spatial reasoning, and geometric modeling to solve problems.

Spend a Million

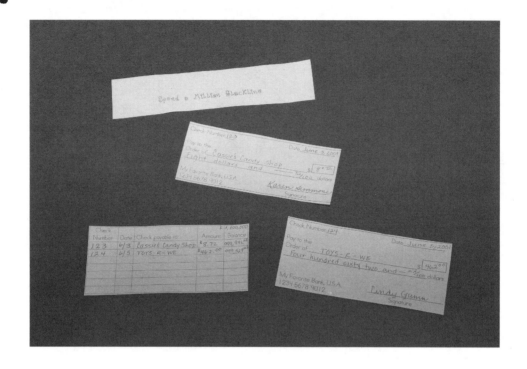

Materials

1. Catalogs and newspapers that include price listings
2. Calculator (optional)
3. Pencils
4. Blackline master 19 for checkbook, or ask a bank to donate temporary checks.

Extensions

*Have the students research terms associated with banking such as *deposit, withdraw, account, borrow, lend,* and *interest.*

*If possible invite a banker to your classroom, or take a field trip to a local bank.

Procedures

1. Read aloud the section of the story *If You Made a Million* that deals with writing a check.

2. Explain to them that they have just won $1,000,000 and must decide what to buy.

3. Give each child multiple copies of the blackline master to make a checkbook.

4. Using the catalogs and newspapers they may begin spending their money. With each purchase they must write out a check from their checkbook.

5. Ask them to keep a journal of all purchases and explain why they made those choices.

6. They must also deduct the amounts from the check register that they spent.

NOTE-If the students are not familiar with the check-writing process, create a check on a overhead transparency or on chart paper.

Magic Touch

*Have someone come to your classroom door and present the class with their winnings. Make the presentation special with balloons and an oversided check, like that of a sweepstakes winner.

*Students can also design a checkbook cover to hold their checks and check registers.

NCTM Standards

PROBLEM SOLVING
Standard-The students will build new mathematical knowledge through problem solving.

Standard-The students will apply and adapt a variety of appropriate strategies to solve problems.

CONNECTIONS
Standard-The students will recognize and apply mathematics in contexts outside of mathematics.

Symmetry Paint Pictures

Materials

1. One 8-1/2-inch by 11-inch sheet of white drawing paper
2. Tempera paint in a variety of colors
3. Paint brushes
4. Black fine-tip marker

Extensions

*Cut pictures from a magazine, then cut them in half. Have the students glue half of the picture to a piece of drawing paper, and draw the other half of the picture to show symmetry.

Procedures

1. Create and paint a symmetrical design with a folded sheet of paper.

2. Fold the sheet of 8-1/2-inch by 11-inch sheet of drawing paper in half horizontally. (We call this a hamburger fold.)

3. Open the folded drawing paper and dab tempera paint near the fold on one side of the paper.

4. Refold the paper on the fold line and rub the outside of the paper to transfer the paint to the other side of the paper.

5. Open your paper and allow paint to dry completely.

6. Once paint is dried, use a fine-tip marker to add details that make the symmetrical paint blobs into a object.

NOTE: Remind the students to try to keep both sides of their illustrations symmetrical when drawing the black outline.

Magic Touch

*Follow this project with a writing activity using the following prompt:

"Look at your symmetrical project design. What does it look like? Add a background and write about it." Display pictures and stories to be shared with others.

NCTM Standards

GEOMETRY
Standard-The students will apply transformations and use symmetry to analyze mathematical situations.

Standard-The students will use visualization, spatial reasoning, and geometric modeling to solve problems.

PROBLEM SOLVING
Standard-The students will build new mathematical knowledge through problem solving

Velcro Math Poems

Materials

1. One 8-1/2-inch by 11-inch white drawing paper
2. Scraps of different colors of construction paper
3. Velcro dots or small, cut pieces of velcro
4. Scissors
5. Crayons, colored pencils or markers

Extensions

*Put the students' poems into a class book and place it in your math center for the students to practice identifying geometric shapes.

Procedures

Magic Touch

1. Begin by creating a chart of geometric shapes. Ask students to brainstorm words that rhyme with the shapes they have listed.

2. Have students as a class or individually create a poem about one of the listed shapes.

3. Each student then may choose a shape to illustrate. When he/she chooses a shape poem, he/she should keep in mind he/she will be using that shape to create their illustrations.

EXAMPLE: If a student selects the circle, he should include as many things as he can that are in the shape of a circle to go along with the poem. (pizza, ball, button etc.)

4. Using the scraps of construction paper the students should cut out their chosen shapes in the same size as in their picture. Then finish the picture by attaching these shapes with Velcro to the proper place in their pictures.

*Have the students use felt scraps, Fun Foam scraps or tagboard to make their attachable shapes. Challenge others to try and attach the shapes to their proper place in each picture.

NCTM Standards

GEOMETRY
Standard-The students will specify locations and describe spatial relationships using coordinate geometry and other representational systems.

Standard-The students will apply transformations and use symmetry to analyze mathematical situations.

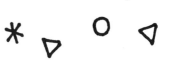

The Magic of Pulling it All Together

If you remember, at the beginning of the book I said it would have taken magic for me to be able to solve word problems in elementary school. I often think that if only I had been taught math with manipulatives and projects, I might have been able to "pull it all together" and use critical thinking skills to explain how to solve problems. I might have been motivated by great literature to learn more about a skill and take more risks to try harder. Most of all, it might have made math fun and less bewildering. The magic we've created for you in the previous two parts helps many students--who like me--found traditionally taught math difficult to understand.

One way we get students involved in learning the vocabulary of math is through a math alphabet book. (See A-B-C Book Blacklines, at end of this book.) Use these blacklines or choose your own vocabulary geared to your students. Drawings are provided for the visual learner, and these can be decorated with colored pencils.

As you use these projects to master the math standards, you need a place for your students to store them. We have included the directions for making folder-holders for each student in our project section. Each pocket will hold the many activities, writing, and vocabulary books that make learning math a subject that can be reviewed and remembered.

We've talked about the magic of literature as motivator. We've discussed the magic of the activities and projects as fun and creative parts of math that enlist a child's senses to master the skills. We've helped students write about math and keep journals to explain problem solving. We have made manipulative managers to store some of the tools.

But the real magic is *you*, the teacher! You are the one who truly guides that struggling math student to achieve, that above-average math student to be challenged, and that average math student to stay motivated and progressing. *You* are the most important part of *this* equation. Your enthusiasm, support, and encouragement, help all students to learn and take risks in math. By loving what you do and making math hands-on and fun, you help your students meet the demands of an ever-changing math curriculum.

For some extra help, we have included the directions for a magic wand. And now for the magic...as you teach math, wave this wand and mention three compliments and a wish. "I liked the way you used vocabulary to explain the problem. I liked the way you tried to work the problem. I liked the way you wrote your letters neatly. I *wish* you would do all of your written homework this well!"

Students can also make their own magic wands to use as pointers for word walls.

We sincerely hope that we have helped you to teach math the way your students need to learn it: in a print-rich environment, with good activities and projects, great literature, exciting writing prompts, many manipulatives, and a sprinkling of magic!

Folder Holder

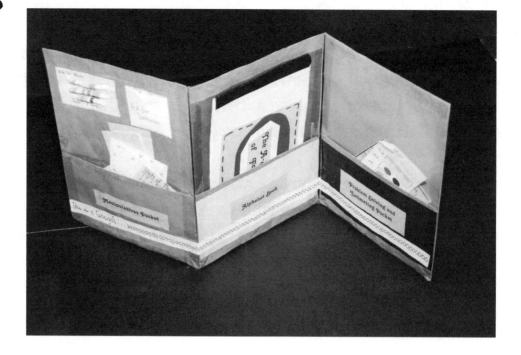

Materials

1. Three large brown grocery bags
2. Three sheets of construction paper, 9-inch by 12-inch
3. Clear-wide tape with dispenser
4. Scissors
5. Markers
6. Ruler
7. Glue

Extensions

*We have found these folders are great for other projects also. For science, label the pockets "Study Sheets," "Experiments," and "Writing." For writing, "Rough Drafts," "Editing," and "Published." For reading, "Characters," "Settings," and "My Stories."

Procedures

1. Place one bag with the flap at the bottom in front of you. Fold flap down toward the bottom of the bag.

2. Using a ruler, draw a line the width of the ruler down the left side of the bag, 12 inches long. Repeat this step down the right side of the bag. Then connect the two lines across the bottom.

3. Cut along these lines, cutting through the top sheet of bag only. Save this cut-away piece for other projects.

4. Open the bag so it sits up. Cut from the front of the bag around to the side but not through the back. Repeat on the other side of bag.

5. Collapse the bag to the original position. Glue a sheet of construction paper into the bag horizontally, folding the excess at the top of the bag down over the construction paper. Glue into place.

6. Repeat steps 1-5 with the other two bags.

7. Lay the first bag face to face with the second bag so bottom flaps are touching. Tape left sides together. Open and tape on inside of bag. Lay the third bag face down on the second bag and tape right sides together. Open and tape on the inside.

8. Tape down outside edges to secure pockets. Open folder and label each pocket. To close, fold one side to middle, then fold other side to middle.

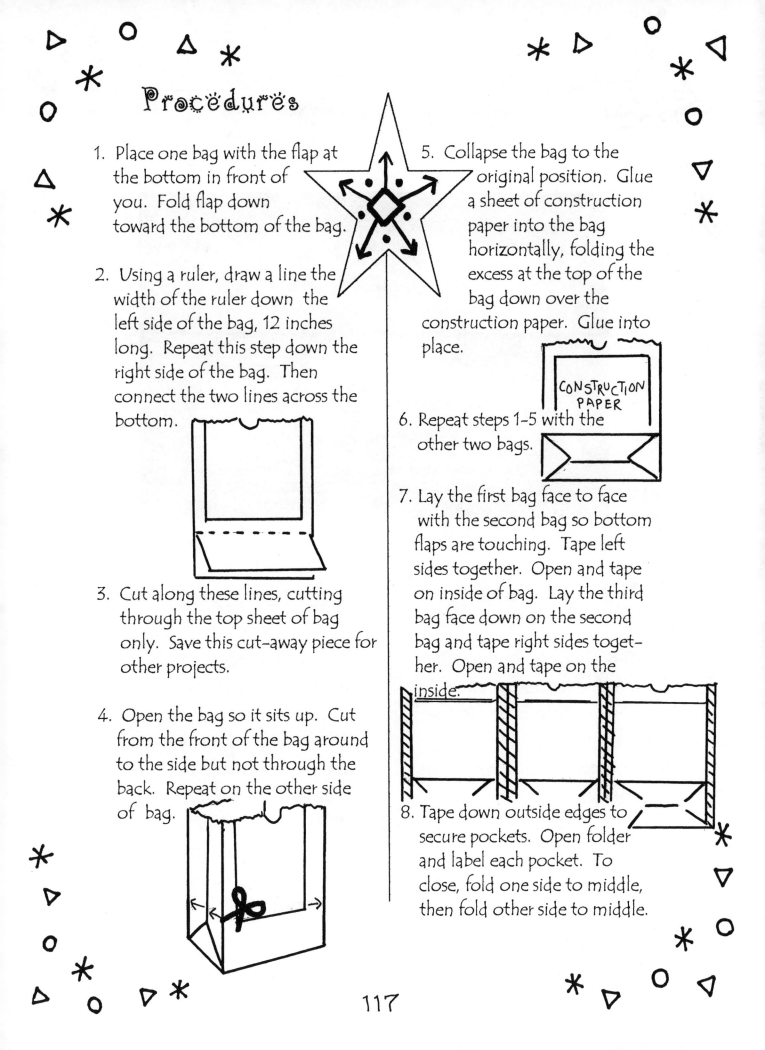

117

A-B-C Book

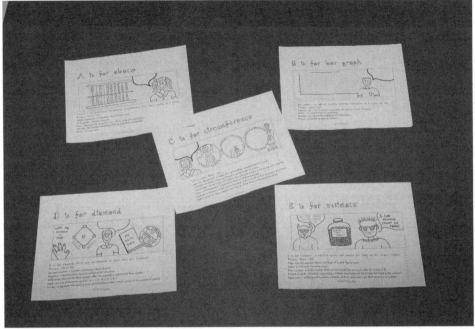

Materials

1. A-B-C Book blackline 20
2. One file folder for cover
3. Three or four brass fasteners
4. Hole puncher
5. Crayons, colored pencils or markers

Extensions

*The A-B-C Book can be made along with the Folder Holder project. Store the book in one of the pockets while the students are working on it. It's a great way to keep the students organize while working on a long-term project.

Procedures

1. Complete each blackline master by adding grade-appropriate vocabulary either from the provided vocabulary list or from a list you create for your students. The students can also define each word by looking up the definition or putting the definition in their own words.

2. The students can create their own illustrations for each letter, or they can color and complete the A to Z illustrations provided. If you use the provided illustrations, have the students fill in the character bubble to match the words provided.

   EXAMPLE: A is for Abacus
   Caption-It's hard to believe some people can add as quickly on an abacus as they can on a calculator.

3. To bind your A-B-C book, punch three or four holes in the left edge of the paper and the file folder. Then secure with the brass fasteners. Now, decorate the cover.

Magic Touch

*Complete the project over a 6 to 9 week period, allowing the students to work on it from time to time. If you try to complete it all at one time the students will not show the same quality in their work. We used this project over an entire school year along with our regular math textbook.

NCTM Standards

CONNECTIONS
Standard-The students will recognize and use connections among mathematical ideas.

Standard-The students understand how mathematical ideas interconnect and build on one another to produce a coherent whole.

Standard-The students will recognize and apply mathematics in contexts outside of mathematics.

Math-Literature Reports

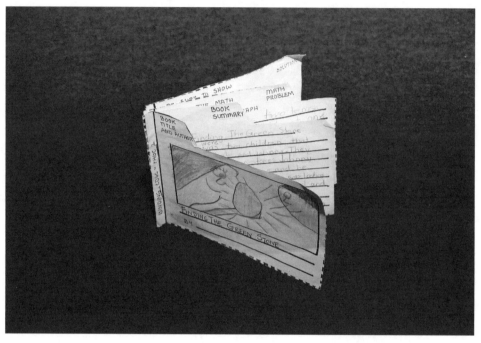

Materials

1. One copy of blackline master 20
2. Scissors
3. Crayons, colored pencils or markers
4. Stapler or tape to bind

Extensions

*Have students keep this type of report in a recipe box or at a learning center.

*Math comes alive when it is connected to literature. Have students read a story and then create math problems that relate to it.

Procedures

1. Cut apart the Blackline master 20 along the dotted lines.

2. Cut away the slashed area on pages 1, 2, and 3, making each page resemble a recipe card.

3. Sequence the pages into the proper order and staple or tape together.

4. Complete information on each page and share with others.

Explain to students

Did you know some books have a lot of math in them? The math often doesn't look like the kind in a math book. Think about the story, events, and characters. Use this information to make up your own math problems about the story.

Example: *A Cloak for the Dreamer* Use geometric shapes to create a different type of cloak than the one designed in the story. See how many different shapes you can use, and label them with their mathematical name.

Magic Touch

*Be sure to model this type of book report to your students before you expect them to try it on their own.

*Copy Blackline master 20 to colored paper so each page of the report is in a different color. This will add some pizzazz to their projects.

NCTM Standard

PROBLEM SOLVING
Standard-The students will build new mathematical knowledge through problem solving.

Standard-The students will solve problems that arise in mathematics and in other contexts.

Standard-The students will apply and adapt a variety of appropriate strategies to solve problems.

Math Journaling

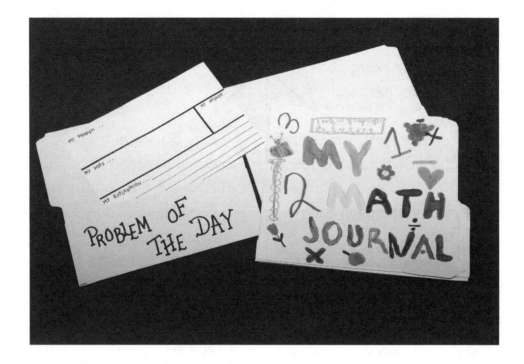

Materials

1. Two file folders
2. Scotch tape
3. Scissors
4. Black fine-tip marker

Extensions

*Use math journals starting at kindergarten.

*Try giving the students a problem each morning when they come into class.

*Begin by modeling problems together, slowly working them to independence.

Procedures

1. Fold up the bottom of each file folder by 3-1/2 inches toward the middle of the folder.

2. Cut off the tabs if they don't match up and use Scotch tape to close the end of each pocket. Refold each folder at center fold.

3. Cut away the folded edge one inch in from either end of one folder(We call this a window). Set this folder aside.

4. Using second folder cut a 1-inch slit in each end of the folder at the folded edge.

5. Fold folder with the slits in half vertically so the slits are in the middle but do not crease. Hold page with the window in the other hand and insert through the window.

Magic Touch

*Have students label each pocket of their their math journal for different types of problems. Examples of labels:
-Problem of the Day
-Estimating Problems
-My Favorite Math Problems
-Math/Literature Reports

*See the Bag Ladies Blackline masters for additional ideas.

NCTM Standards

NUMBERS AND OPERATIONS
Standard-The students will compute fluently and make reasonable estimations.

PROBLEM SOLVING
Standard-The students will build new mathematical knowledge through problem-solving.

COMMUNICATIONS
Standard-The students will use the language of mathematics to express mathematical ideas precisely.

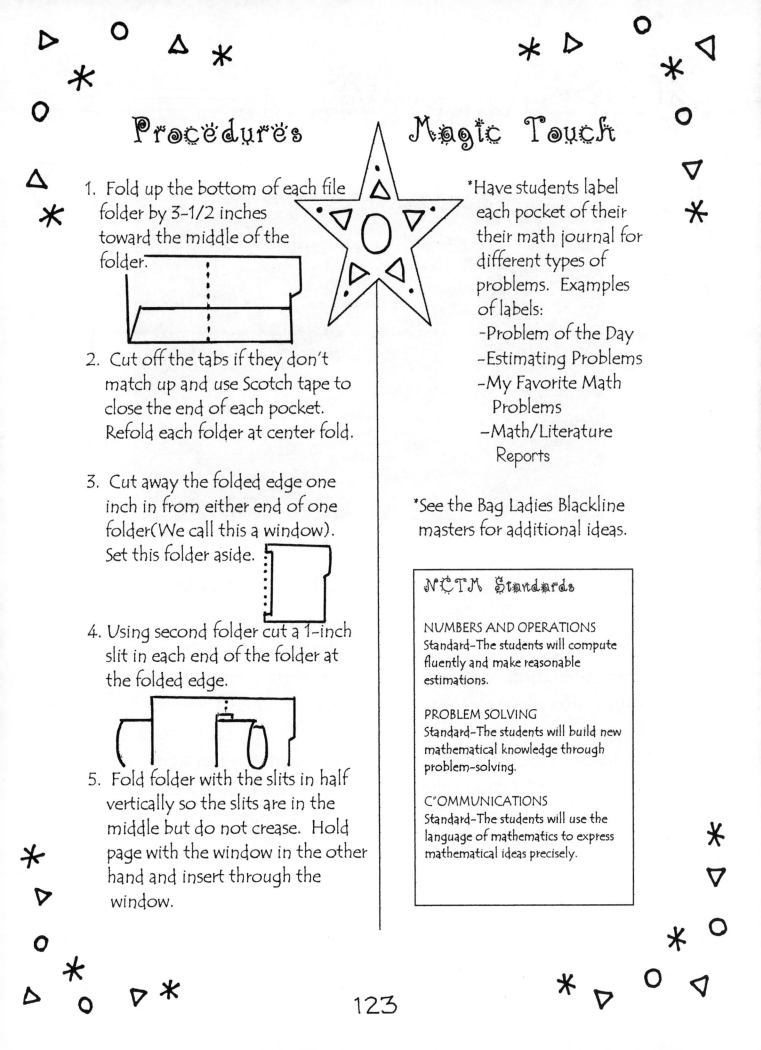

Magic Wands

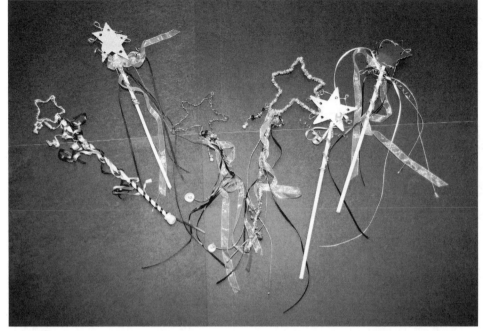

Materials

1. One star cut from corragated cardboard
2. One glittery pipe cleaner
3. One 3/8-inch dowel rod 12 to 18-inches in length
4. One yard of 22 gauge wire
5. Two 12-inch lengths of curling ribbon
6. Hole puncher

Extensions

*Use magic wands as props for stories, behavior modi-fication, or as a pointer.
*Have the students create their own magic wands with art center materials and craft supplies brought from home.

Procedures

1. Begin by punching holes in each point of the cardboard star.

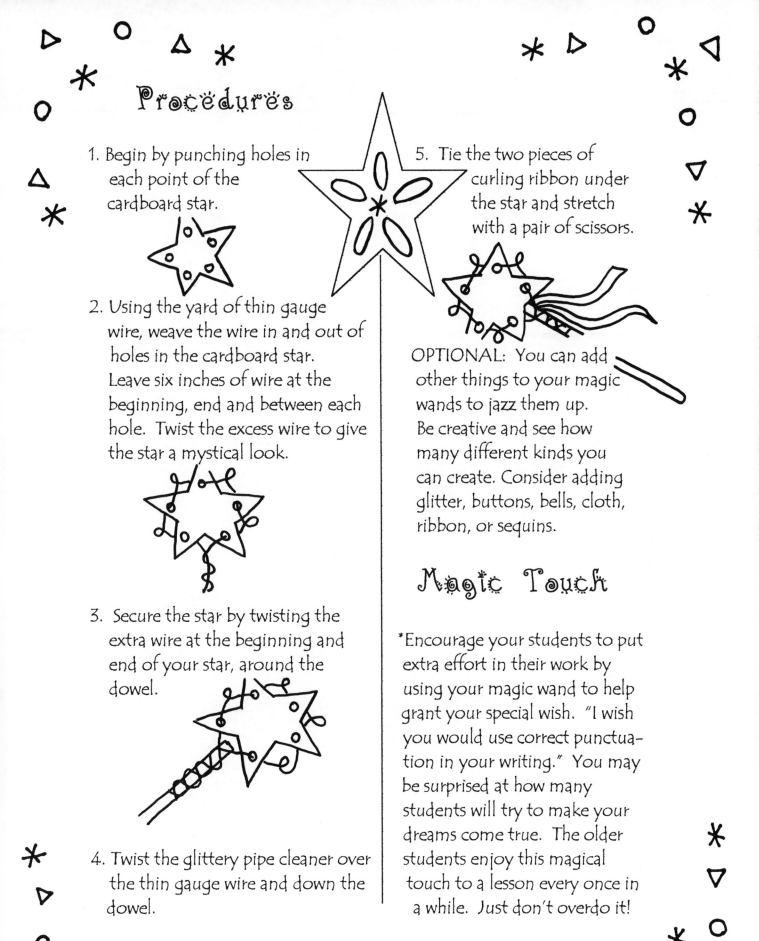

2. Using the yard of thin gauge wire, weave the wire in and out of holes in the cardboard star. Leave six inches of wire at the beginning, end and between each hole. Twist the excess wire to give the star a mystical look.

3. Secure the star by twisting the extra wire at the beginning and end of your star, around the dowel.

4. Twist the glittery pipe cleaner over the thin gauge wire and down the dowel.

5. Tie the two pieces of curling ribbon under the star and stretch with a pair of scissors.

OPTIONAL: You can add other things to your magic wands to jazz them up. Be creative and see how many different kinds you can create. Consider adding glitter, buttons, bells, cloth, ribbon, or sequins.

Magic Touch

*Encourage your students to put extra effort in their work by using your magic wand to help grant your special wish. "I wish you would use correct punctuation in your writing." You may be surprised at how many students will try to make your dreams come true. The older students enjoy this magical touch to a lesson every once in a while. Just don't overdo it!

Domino Blackline 1A

128

Domino Blackline 1B

Domino Blackline 1C

© 2001 The Bag Ladies

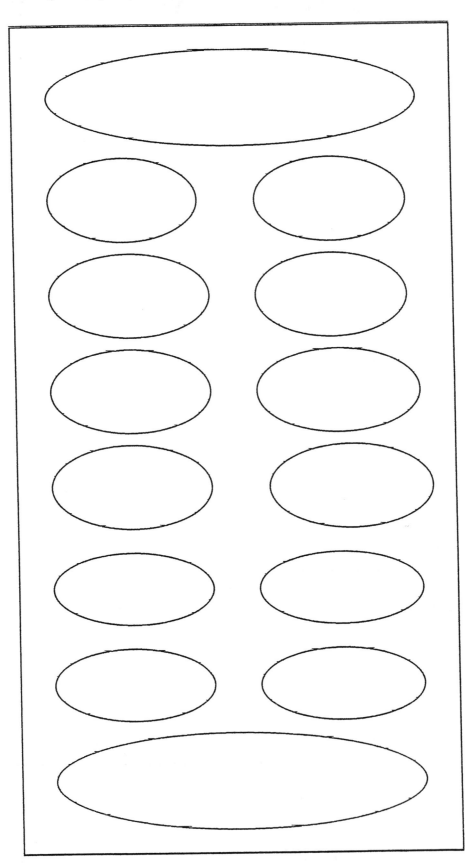

Estimating Jar Count

	100's	10's	1's
Items in jar_____ My guess_____ Total_____			

	100's	10's	1's
Items in jar_____ My guess_____ Total_____			

	100's	10's	1's
Items in jar_____ My guess_____ Total_____			

	100's	10's	1's
Items in jar_____ My guess_____ Total_____			

	100's	10's	1's
Items in jar_____ My guess_____ Total_____			

Problem Solving-Blackline 5

My Problem

My Work

My Explanation

My Answer

Candy Bar Fractions Blackline 6
Page 1

___ / 12	CUT AWAY	CUT AWAY	CUT AWAY	HERSHEY	CUT AWAY	CUT AWAY	CUT AWAY
CUT AWAY	CUT AWAY	CUT AWAY	CUT AWAY	___ = ___ / 12	CUT AWAY	CUT AWAY	CUT AWAY
CUT AWAY	CUT AWAY	CUT AWAY	CUT AWAY	CUT AWAY	CUT AWAY	CUT AWAY	CUT AWAY
HERSHEY	CUT AWAY	CUT AWAY	CUT AWAY	HERSHEY	___ = ___ / 12	CUT AWAY	CUT AWAY
HERSHEY	CUT AWAY	CUT AWAY	CUT AWAY	HERSHEY	CUT AWAY	CUT AWAY	CUT AWAY
___ = ___ / 12	CUT AWAY	CUT AWAY	CUT AWAY	HERSHEY	CUT AWAY	CUT AWAY	CUT AWAY
HERSHEY	HERSHEY	CUT AWAY	CUT AWAY	HERSHEY	HERSHEY	CUT AWAY	CUT AWAY
HERSHEY	___ / 12	CUT AWAY	CUT AWAY	HERSHEY	HERSHEY	CUT AWAY	CUT AWAY
HERSHEY	CUT AWAY	CUT AWAY	CUT AWAY	HERSHEY	___ = ___ / 12	CUT AWAY	CUT AWAY

135

Candy Bar Fractions Blackline 6
Page 2

HERSHEY	HERSHEY	$\frac{\quad}{12}$	CUT AWAY	HERSHEY	HERSHEY	HERSHEY	CUT AWAY
HERSHEY	HERSHEY	CUT AWAY	CUT AWAY	HERSHEY	HERSHEY	$\frac{\quad}{12} = \frac{\quad}{\quad}$	CUT AWAY
HERSHEY	HERSHEY	CUT AWAY	CUT AWAY	HERSHEY	HERSHEY	CUT AWAY	CUT AWAY
HERSHEY	HERSHEY	HERSHEY	CUT AWAY	HERSHEY	HERSHEY	HERSHEY	$\frac{\quad}{12} = \frac{\quad}{\quad}$
HERSHEY	HERSHEY	HERSHEY	CUT AWAY	HERSHEY	HERSHEY	HERSHEY	CUT AWAY
HERSHEY	HERSHEY	$\frac{\quad}{12} = \frac{\quad}{\quad}$	CUT AWAY	HERSHEY	HERSHEY	HERSHEY	CUT AWAY
HERSHEY	HERSHEY	HERSHEY	HERSHEY	HERSHEY	HERSHEY	HERSHEY	HERSHEY
HERSHEY	HERSHEY	HERSHEY	$\frac{\quad}{12}$	HERSHEY	HERSHEY	HERSHEY	HERSHEY
HERSHEY	HERSHEY	HERSHEY	CUT AWAY	HERSHEY	HERSHEY	HERSHEY	$\frac{\quad}{12} = $

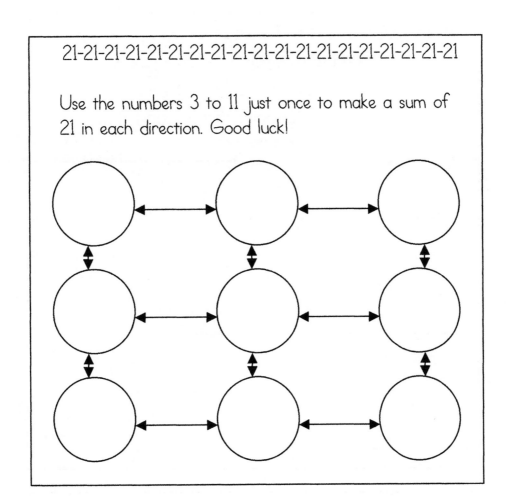

21-21-21-21-21-21-21-21-21-21-21-21-21-21-21-21-21-21-21

Use the numbers 3 to 11 just once to make a sum of 21 in each direction. Good luck!

3	4	5	6	7	8	9	10	11

Answer: 4 – 11 – 6
         9 – 7 – 5
         8 – 3 – 10

Directions: Complete the squares using the numbers 1-2-3-4-5 just once in each row and column to make a sum of 15 going across and down.

1	2	3	4	5	1	2	3	4	5	1	2	3

4	5	1	2	3	4	5	1	2	3	4	5

Answer:

1	2	3	4	5
2	3	4	5	1
3	4	5	1	2
4	5	1	2	3
5	1	2	3	4

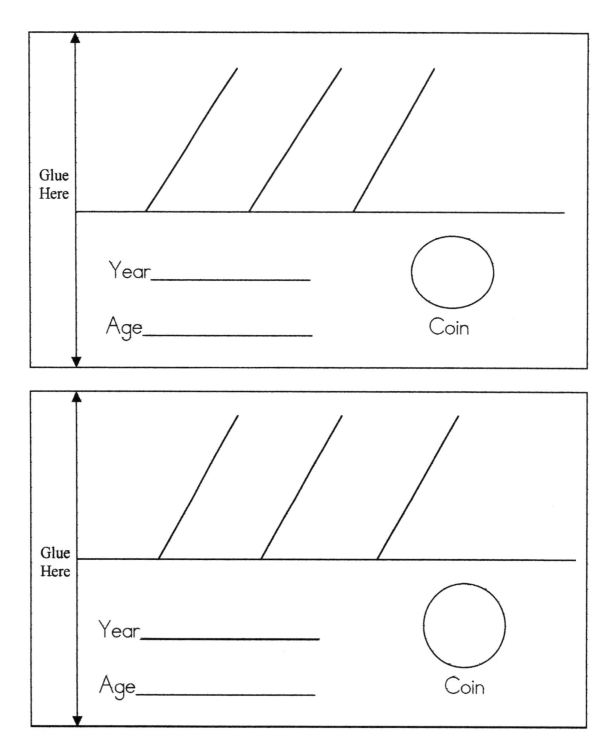

Quilt Patterns 11

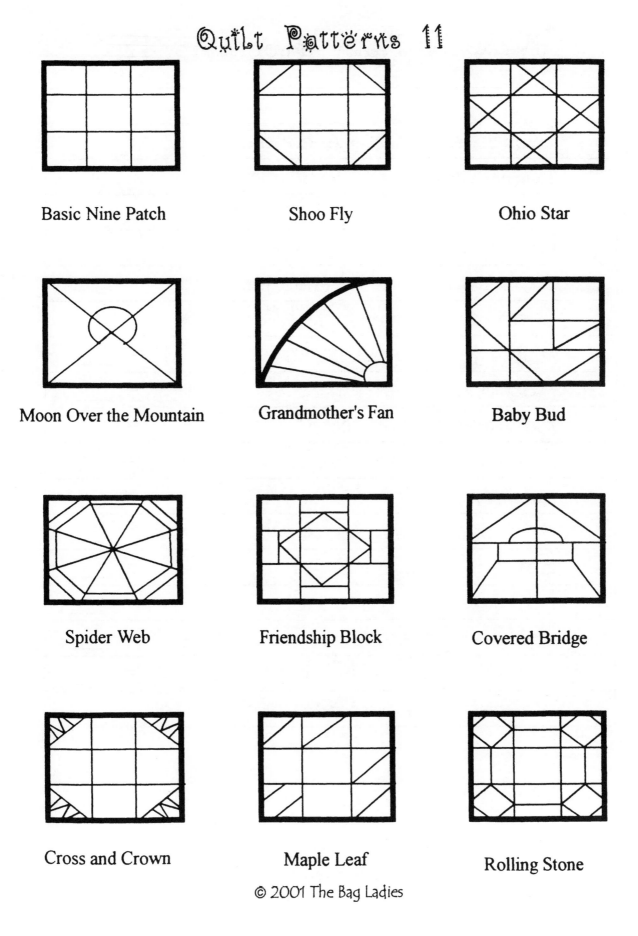

Basic Nine Patch

Shoo Fly

Ohio Star

Moon Over the Mountain

Grandmother's Fan

Baby Bud

Spider Web

Friendship Block

Covered Bridge

Cross and Crown

Maple Leaf

Rolling Stone

One blue M & M candy
Two green M & M candies
Three orange M & M candies
Four yellow M & M candies
Five red M & M candies
Six brown M & M candies
Keep six brown M & M's
Add one blue M & M $6 + 1 = $ ___
Add one green M & M $7 + 1 = $ ___
Add one red M & M $8 + 1 = $ ___
Add one orange M & M $9 + 1 = $ ___
Add one yellow M & M $10 + 1 = $ ___
Add one brown M & M $11 + 1 = $ ___
Eat one blue M & M $12 - 1 = $ ___
Eat seven brown candies $11 - 7 = $ ___
Eat one green M & M $4 - 1 = $ ___
Eat one orange M & M $3 - 1 = $ ___
Now eat the rest of your candies!

Sort the candies by color

Estimate the total number ____

Make a bar graph by color

Add the numbers together

Compare estimate to actual number

Find the difference

Eat one of each color

Divide by 2--one for me, one for you

Any remaining? Eat odd one!

Make four groups of ten

Ten groups of two

Two groups of ten

Divide 4 sets of 10 to 8 sets

Place one of each color in a line

Eat fourth first, fifth second

Eat third third, second fourth

Eat sixth fifth, first last

The End

By _____

Create a Tangram Story 13

*Create a main character using your tangrams. Create a simple drawing in the box to represent this character.

*Use your tangrams to make a puzzle that represents a main event or setting in your story.

*If there are any other main events, places or characters you want to include, use your tangram shapes to create them.

*Don't forget a story ending. Use your tangrams to make a puzzle that represents a part of the ending.

Remember do not overlap or cross pieces over each other when creating your shapes.

Math Wallet Blackline 14

About the Author

Title_____

Author_____

fold | here

Major Events

Story Setting

Story Summary

© 2001 The Bag Ladies

149

_____'s Amazing

Math Dream

Napier Bone Blackline 16

	1	2	3	4	5	6	7	8	9	0
1	1	2	3	4	5	6	7	8	9	0
2	2	4	6	8	10	12	14	16	18	0
3	3	6	9	12	15	18	21	24	27	0
4	4	8	12	16	20	24	28	32	36	0
5	5	10	15	20	25	30	35	40	45	0
6	6	12	18	24	30	36	42	48	54	0
7	7	14	21	28	35	42	49	56	63	0
8	8	16	24	32	40	48	56	64	72	0
9	9	18	27	36	45	54	63	72	81	0

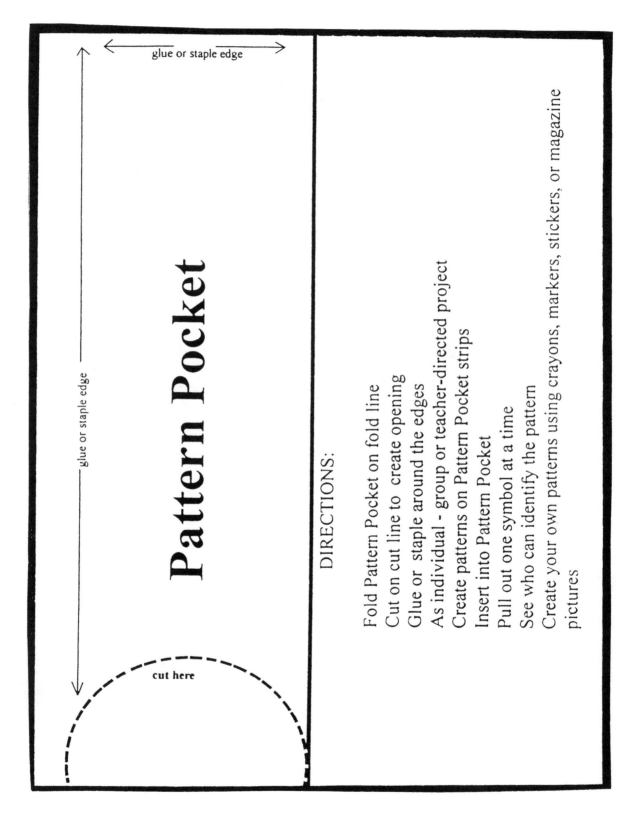

Pattern Pocket

glue or staple edge

glue or staple edge

cut here

DIRECTIONS:

Fold Pattern Pocket on fold line
Cut on cut line to create opening
Glue or staple around the edges
As individual - group or teacher-directed project
Create patterns on Pattern Pocket strips
Insert into Pattern Pocket
Pull out one symbol at a time
See who can identify the pattern
Create your own patterns using crayons, markers, stickers, or magazine pictures

Percent Pattern Grid Paper
BlackLine Master 18

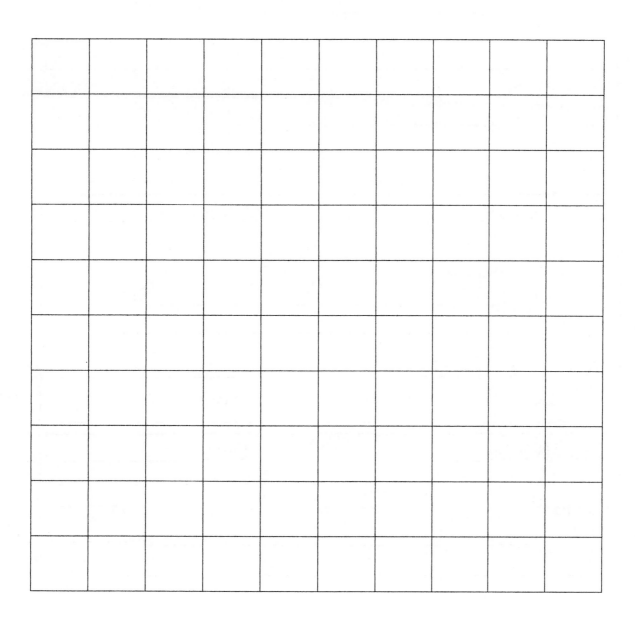

Check Number	Date	Check payable to:	Amount	Balance

Check Number____   Date_____

Pay to the
Order of_____$ [____]
_____dollars

My Favorite Bank, U.S.A.   _____
1234 5678 9012   Signature

Check Number____   Date_____

Pay to the
Order of_____$ [____]
_____dollars

                                                    _____
My Favorite Bank, U.S.A.   Signature
1234 5678 9012

State a math problem that goes along with your story. Write the problem in sentence or paragraph form.

Math Problem

Cut away

_____

_____

_____

_____

_____

_____

_____

Be sure to show your work and explain how you got your answer.

Solution

Explain your answer _____

_____

_____

My answer is _____

Math and Literature Blackline 20

Book and Author

Cut away this area

S
T
A
P
L
E

H
E
R
E

Report created by _____

Summary

Cut away this area

Book title _____

_____
_____
_____
_____
_____
_____

©2001 The Bag Ladies

156

A-B-C Book

blackline masters

_____ is for ___

A is for abacus

B is for bar graph

C is for circumference

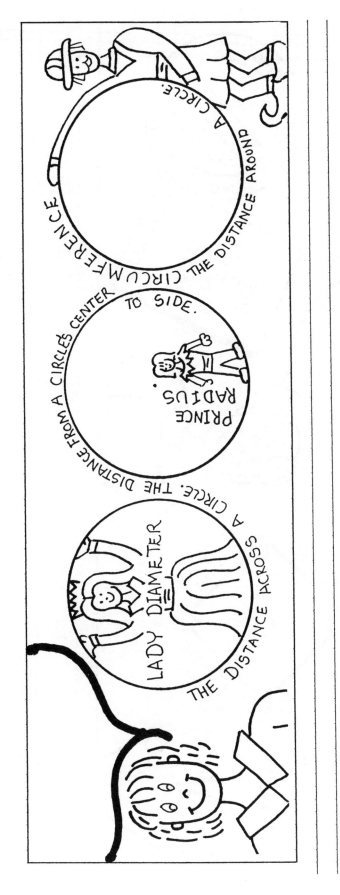

PRINCE RADIUS. THE DISTANCE FROM A CIRCLE'S CENTER TO SIDE.

CIRCUMFERENCE THE DISTANCE AROUND A CIRCLE.

LADY DIAMETER THE DISTANCE ACROSS A CIRCLE.

D is for diamond

NO DIAMONDS

RHOMBUS ONLY

NO DIAMONDS

MY MATH BOOK

THERE ARE DIAMONDS IN BASEBALL.

THERE ARE DIAMONDS IN RINGS.

E is for estimate

F is for Fibonacci

OUR NEW NUMBER SYSTEM, NO MORE ROMAN NUMERALS.

I = 1	VI = 6
II = 2	VII = 7
III = 3	VIII = 8
IV = 4	IX = 9
V = 5	X = 10

FIBONACCI NUMBER SEQUENCE

1 1 2 3 5 8
13 21 34 55
89 144

What comes next?

G is for Googol

If Edward Kasner would have asked me I would of called it a 'GA-GA'.

1 Googol

10,000,000,000,000,000,000,
000,000,000,000,000,000,000,
000,000,000,000,000,000,
000,000,000,000,000,000,000,
000,000,000,000.

H is for hundred

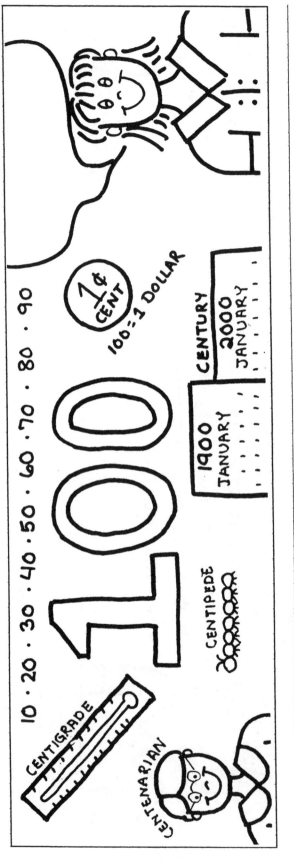

10 · 20 · 30 · 40 · 50 · 60 · 70 · 80 · 90

100

1¢ CENT

100 = 1 DOLLAR

CENTURY

1900 JANUARY

2000 JANUARY

CENTIPEDE

CENTIGRADE

CENTENARIAN

I is for "it"

If you filled a swimming pool full of ice cream how long would it take you to eat it all?

If someone gave you a dollar for every math problem you have gotten right, how much money would you have?

J is for Jupiter

K is for Konigsberg Bridge

BRIDGE TO KONIGSBERG

169

L is for Line Graph

HAPPY :-) ←———→ SAD :-(

7:00 AM · 8:00 · 9:00 · 10:00 · 11:00 · 12:00 · 1:00 PM · 2:00 · 3:00 · 4:00 · 5:00 · 6:00

M is for multiply

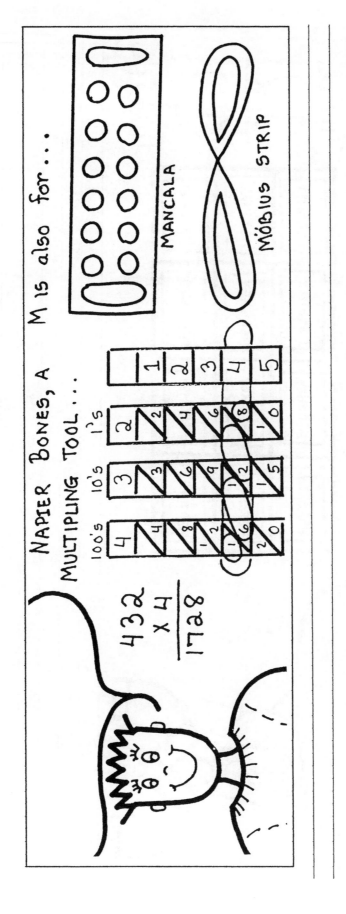

M is also for...

MANCALA

MÖBIUS STRIP

NAPIER BONES, A MULTIPLING TOOL...

$$\begin{array}{r} 432 \\ \times\ 4 \\ \hline 1728 \end{array}$$

N is for numerator

Twelve

$$\frac{12}{12}$$

Twelfths

HERSHEY HERSHEY HERSHEY HERSHEY
HERSHEY HERSHEY HERSHEY HERSHEY
HERSHEY HERSHEY HERSHEY HERSHEY

O is for obtuse

ACUTE →

OBTUSE →

VERY ACUTE →

OBTUSE →

10 20 30 40 50 60 70 80 90 100 110

P is for pizza pie percents

100% CHANCE OF SUNSHINE

100% A+

NAME
DATE
READING

10%
20%
30%
40%
50%
60%
70%
80%
90%
100%

23% RED   1% BROWN
4% GREEN   72% BLUE
= 100 %

Q is for quadrilateral

QUADRILATERALS

NOT QUADRILATERALS

R is for ratio

1 PART : 1 PART = Orange
RED : YELLOW

4 PARTS RED = LAVENDER
1 PART BLUE

3 PARTS BLUE : 2 PARTS YELLOW = GREEN

S is for symmetry

SYMMETRY SAM

LINES OF SYMMETRY

SYMMETRY PICTURE

A CIRCLE HAS AN INFINITE NUMBER OF LINES OF SYMMETRY.

T is for tessellate/tangram

Rabbit

Dog

U is for unit

1 liter

1 Hand

1 foot

A MEASURING STICK

1 CUP

1 yard

179

V is for Venn diagram

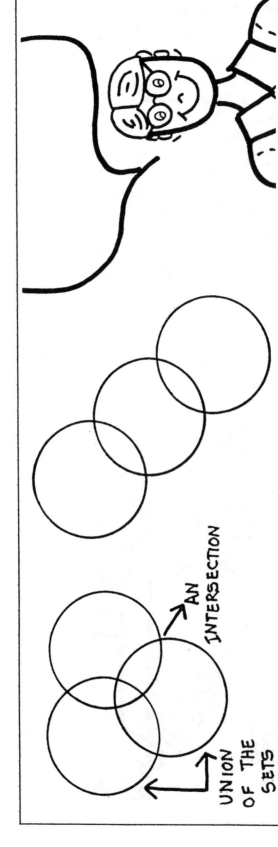

AN INTERSECTION

UNION OF THE SETS

W is for "when Math?"

THINGS YOU NEED MATH TO MAKE...

BUILDINGS BIG & SMALL

BRIDGES

ROADS

GAMES THAT USE MATH...

TIC-TAC-TOE

MANCALA

CHECKERS

MARBLES

X is for "=x"

x^{100} = one googol

x^{googol} = one googolplex

$12 - x = 10$

2 wrongs ≠ 1

$3 + 4 = x$

X marks the spot

$2x = 4$

Y is for y-axis

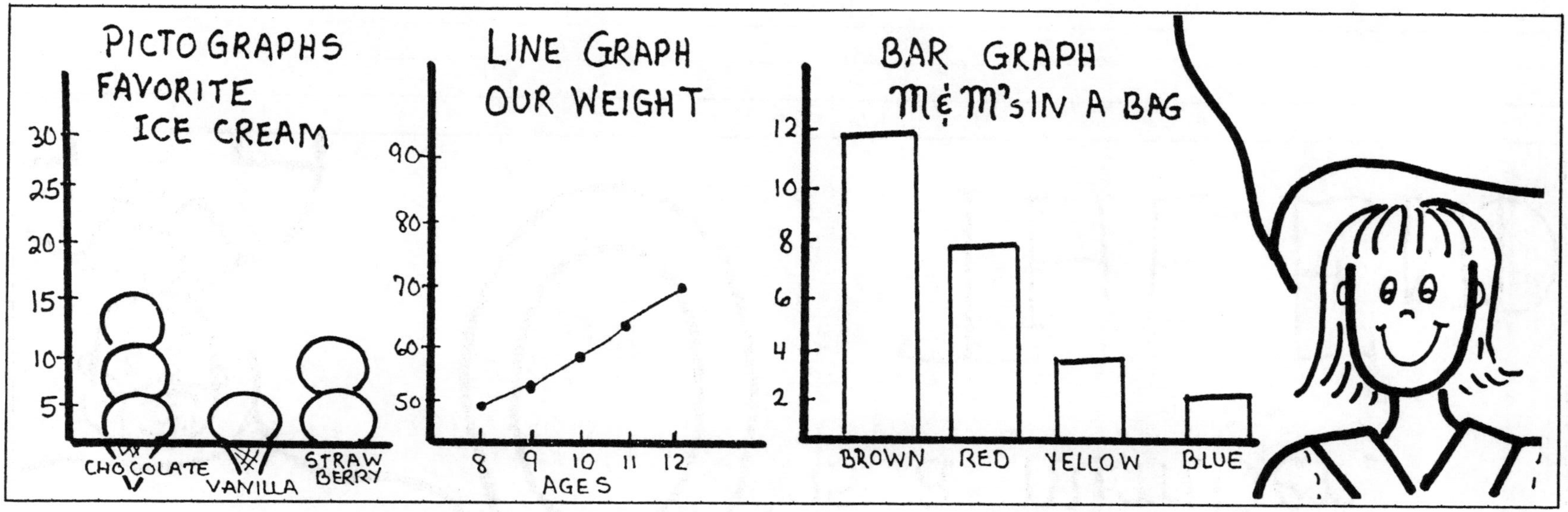

PICTOGRAPHS
FAVORITE ICE CREAM

30
25
20
15
10
5

CHOCOLATE VANILLA STRAW BERRY

LINE GRAPH
OUR WEIGHT

90
80
70
60
50

8 9 10 11 12
AGES

BAR GRAPH
M & M's IN A BAG

12
10
8
6
4
2

BROWN RED YELLOW BLUE

z is for zero

O is a number.

THE END

About the Authors

Cindy Guinn and Karen Simmons presently teach in Palm Beach County, Florida. Between them they have forty years experience and have taught all grades K-6. Both have been recipients of, and nominated for, numerous education awards. They began The Bag Ladies workshops to present an energetic, enthusiastic, creative, motivational, and fun workshop to their teaching peers.

Using their own self-published thematic units, they demonstrate skills, bookmaking ideas, and numerous hands-on projects that can be used in any classroom. Participants make these projects and are able to gear them to their own curriculums and standards.

A Bookbag of the Bag Ladies Best is their first book, culminating their years of teaching, presenting and creating. Their second book, *Math Manipulatives, and Magic Wands*, combines reading, writing, and math in a hands-on format for teachers.

The Bag Ladies demonstrate the art of making learning fun for both teachers and students, while using the state standards to guarantee positive state testing results. Each year participants use these skills to take home a different thematic bag full of ideas that can be used in their own classrooms.

These teachers/authors have presented for numerous years at the Florida Reading Association and the Florida Council for Elementary Education Conference plus all over the United States at various State Reading Council Conferences and schools. They presented to The International Reading Association in New Orleans and the National Math Conference in Orlando. In addition they presented to the National I Teach 1st Conference in California and Orlando.

Watch the Bag Ladies take the stress out of teaching state standards in a hands-on approach to covering those benchmarks all the way to testing day and beyond. They will also add a "sprinkle of magic" to every grade's curriculum.

Bag Ladies' Units Order Form

Quantity	Title	Price	Tax	Total
_____	How Does Your Garden Grow	17.00	1.02	____
_____	Up in the Air	17.00	1.02	____
_____	Lights, Cameras, Shadows, Actions	17.00	1.02	____
_____	Ants, Bats, and Other Creatures	17.00	1.02	____
_____	Kids, Colors, Quilts	17.00	1.02	____
_____	Hats Off to the USA	17.00	1.02	____
_____	Our Classroom Becomes an			
	Ancient Egyptian Museum	17.00	1.02	____
_____	Recycling After the Picnic	17.00	1.02	____
_____	A Walk Across Florida	17.00	1.02	____
_____	Book Talks	17.00	1.02	____
_____	Writing Thoughts	17.00	1.02	____
_____	A Mathsquerade for the			
	Millennium and Beyond	17.00	1.02	____
_____	Readin, Ritin, and Rithmetic	17.00	1.02	____
_____	The Poetry Pouch	17.00	1.02	____
_____ new	Under the Ground, On the Ground,			
	Above the Ground	17.00	1.02	____
_____ new	Positively Perfect Projects	17.00	1.02	____

SUBTOTAL ____

Shipping and handling (10%) ____

TOTAL ____

Mail Order to: Bag Ladies   **Ship to:** Name_____

PMB 256   Address_____

1128 Royal Palm Beach Blvd.   _____

Royal Palm Beach, FL 33411   City_____

State/ zip_____

(561) 793-8268   (561) 463-1420   bagladiesonline.com

NOTES

NOTES